D1094525

DOUGLAS MacARTHUR

LIVES TO REMEMBER

Douglas MacArthur

by Alfred Steinberg

G. P. PUTNAM'S SONS
NEW YORK

© 1961 by Alfred Steinberg

Fifth Impression

Library of Congress Catalog
Card Number: 60-12537

MANUFACTURED IN THE UNITED STATES OF AMERICA

VAN REES PRESS • NEW YORK

Published simultaneously in the Dominion of Canada by
Longmans Canada Limited, Toronto

CONTENTS

For POLLY MOLLY

DOUGLAS MacARTHUR

Chapter 1

MILITARY TRADITION

O NE warm spring morning in 1901, a slim, short, swarthy Filipino named Manuel Luis Quezon arrived in Manila under a flag of truce. Major Quezon had come from the Bataan Peninsula to see General Arthur MacArthur, military governor of the Philippine Islands.

A few years earlier, Quezon had joined other Filipino patriots under the leadership of Emilio Aguinaldo to throw off the hated three-hundred-year yoke of their Spanish rulers. With the help of the United States, which had gone to war with Spain, this was readily accomplished in 1898. However, when the American government in turn insisted upon taking over the 7,083 islands of the Philippine archipelago, Quezon and Aguinaldo set off a fiery war against their liberators.

Now, three years later, General MacArthur held Aguinaldo captive and the insurrection had collapsed. Downhearted but with his penetrating eyes still ablaze, Quezon trudged into Malacanan Palace, the headquarters of the American military governor. Still defiant, he nevertheless surrendered his sword to the mustached, quiet general. Quezon's world seemingly lay in ruin, and his hatred of Americans, as personified by General Arthur MacArthur, overwhelmed him.

Yet time has a way of altering men and opinions. In 1935, some thirty-four years later, Manuel Quezon had risen to the top as President of the newly organized Philippine Commonwealth. By an act of the Congress of the United States, his homeland would become a completely independent nation in 1946.

But on the horizon there stood the menace of an aggressive Japan, hungrily on the march to swallow all of Asia. The Philippines lacked both an army and a preparedness program. Most frightening of all, she lay directly in the path of Japan's ambitions.

With a future so dark, Quezon went to the White House in Washington, D. C., to plead with President Franklin D. Roosevelt for aid. "I want your best general to direct the Commonwealth defenses," he told Roosevelt.

Roosevelt smiled. "And who would that be?"

"The son of General Arthur MacArthur," Quezon said, without hesitation. "General Douglas MacArthur." No other person would do.

When Douglas MacArthur was born in the old Federal Arsenal at Little Rock, Arkansas, on January 26, 1880, he was already part of a proud military tradition. MacArthur clansmen were among the fiercest warriors in ancient Scotland. Some had fought in the Crusades. Others added to the clan's glory by fighting under Robert the Bruce in the successful fourteenth-century struggle for Scots freedom and independence at Bannockburn. These were only some of the gallant, fighting MacArthurs who played top roles in Scottish history for more than one thousand years. All of them pointed with pride to the famous Scots proverb: "There is nothing older, unless the hills—MacArthur and the Devil."

The first MacArthur to arrive in the United States was hardly a warlike man. He was Arthur MacArthur, Douglas MacArthur's grandfather, who came with his widowed mother to Massachusetts in 1830. After schooling at Amherst College, he studied law, served as a military judge, then moved to Wisconsin where he became city attorney of Milwaukee and lieutenant governor. In time he became a close friend to Abraham Lincoln and General Grant and spent his later years in the nation's capital as judge of the District of Columbia Supreme Court.

It was while Judge MacArthur was living in Wisconsin that the MacArthurs reverted to their military tradition. When the Civil War broke out in 1861, the judge's older son, also named Arthur MacArthur, pleaded with his father for permission to join the Union forces. However, since he was still fifteen years old, his father refused to let him go. Furthermore, he employed a detective to make certain that he did not run away.

Nevertheless, young Arthur's constant nagging for permission finally wore down the judge's resistance and in August of 1862 he gave his blessing to his seventeen-year-old son. That same month he watched the lad march away proudly as first lieutenant and adjutant of the soon-to-be-renowned 24th Wisconsin Infantry.

The "Little Adjutant," the men sneeringly called their undersized lieutenant with the high, weak voice. The first time the men were on dress parade and Arthur MacArthur gave the orders, the thousand men roared with laughter at his squeaky commands. Afterward, the colonel shouted that he would write the governor and "demand a man instead of a boy for adjutant."

But Arthur MacArthur showed himself a man instead of a boy once the battle lines were reached. At his first battle at Perryville in Kentucky, he was cited for gallantry. The men of the 24th said of him with awe: "He's the bravest little devil we ever saw."

Then at the bloody battle of Stone River in Tennessee shortly before Christmas in 1862, he emerged as his regiment's hero. General Phil Sheridan took note of him here and became his staunchest admirer. Later at the Battle of Missionary Ridge, during November, 1863, young MacArthur won the coveted Congressional Medal of Honor and came to the attention of General U. S. Grant. His regiment had been ordered to climb the steep, rocky hill and stop at the first line of Confederate trenches. Southern guns raked Missionary Ridge with deadly fire as the men started upward. One color bearer fell and when another man picked up the flag, he, too, was shot down. With a brisk, fearless motion, Lieutenant MacArthur raised the regimental colors, and rushed up the hill onto the Confederate breastworks. In a moment he was past the enemy front line with his loyal men following behind him.

Watching the battle, General Grant gulped and shouted to his aide, "Why don't they stop at that position?"

"When those fellows get started, sir," came the reply, "nothing can stop them."

"Well," Grant grumbled, "it will be all right if it turns out all right."

The battle was won and Lieutenant MacArthur's heroism became a part of Army folklore. There were no objections when he advanced to the rank of major at eighteen and to colonel at twenty when the Civil War ended.

When the Reconstruction period began, the "Boy Colonel of the West" was mustered out of service. But he was so determined to make his career in the Army that he returned to service in 1866 as a second lieutenant of infantry. He married a pretty Southern belle named Mary Pinkney Hardy, though four of her brothers who had served in the Confederate forces refused to attend the wedding.

Then began a life at Army posts on the raw Western frontier. In 1876, their first son, Arthur, was born. The next year came Malcolm, who died a few years later of measles. Finally on a cold January day of 1880, on his grandfather's sixty-fifth birthday, came Douglas.

Chapter 2

ARMY BRAT

My earliest memory," said Douglas MacArthur years later, "is the sound of Army bugles."

The American Army in the post-Civil War period was devoting much of its efforts to holding angry Indian tribes in check as hordes of settlers rumbled westward deep into Indian territory. Captain MacArthur took his wife and two sons wherever he went, and for long periods of time little Douglas lived in lonely forts amid continual danger. "When I was a little boy of four," he recalled, "my father was a captain in the 13th Infantry, stationed at Fort Selden in the Indian frontier of New Mexico. Geronimo, the Apache scourge, was loose, and our little infantry garrison was to guard the upper fords of the Rio Grande. A troop of the 5th Cavalry rode through to help us. I can still remember how I felt when I watched them clatter into the fort, their tired horses gray with the desert dust."

His father had a great knack of finding himself in the midst of trouble. There were the surprise hit-and-run Indian Wars in the Utah Territory, centering about Fort Rawlins. Some said he exposed himself needlessly. But he was entirely without fear. On one occasion near Fort Bridger in the Wyoming Territory, his foolhardiness brought him into hand-to-hand combat with war-paint-smeared Indians and he narrowly escaped being scalped.

However, as he pointed out to Douglas, by way of an object lesson, duty and courage were the essential qualities of a good soldier. Besides, the MacArthurs seemed to be blessed with charmed existences in battle. Even a close family relationship could prove an indirect lifesaver, he told his little son. To illustrate this, he noted his experience during one engagement of the Civil War. He had crammed a shirt pocket with a dozen letters from home. This later saved his life, for though an enemy sniper drew a bead on his heart and pressed the trigger, the bullet failed to pierce the thick packet of mail.

There were many heroes of the Old West whom little Douglas came to know. One of the most impressive was Buffalo Bill, whose colorful garb and pointed beard lent him an aura of supreme romance. There were also Western heroes, dead before Douglas was born, whose adventures were brought to life for him by his father who had known them. One of these was "Wild Bill" Hickock, famous Western marshal.

As an aide to General Phil Sheridan, Captain MacArthur told Douglas, he had once accompanied Sheridan for a conference with some Sioux chiefs who were preparing for the warpath. On that occasion, Wild Bill Hickock served as interpreter and the three men sat in a circle with the Indian chieftains. Sheridan hoped to frighten the Indians from their proposed venture.

"Bill," he told Hickock, "I want you to tell these chiefs that they shouldn't fight the white man. He can do things they never heard of. Bill, tell them about the white man's railroad trains. Tell them how it will haul all the buffalo meat three times as fast as their fastest horses can run."

The Indians sneered at this statement and Hickock told Sheridan, "General, they said they don't believe you."

"All right," said Sheridan, "tell them how the white man has invented a big boat that will go without paddles or sails."

Again the Indians grunted disbelief.

General Sheridan looked annoyed. "Well, then, tell them, Bill, about the telegraph. Tell them that I have a little black box out here and the Great White Father has a little black box in Washington. When I talk into my box the Great White Father hears me, and when the Great White Father talks into his box I hear him."

Hickock did not speak. Finally, Sheridan angrily told him to relay the message.

Hickock looked him in the eye and chewed on his wad of tobacco. "General," he finally spoke, "now I don't believe you."

Although Douglas' aristocratic mother had been raised in ease and comfort in a Norfolk, Virginia, mansion and on a North Carolina plantation, she adapted herself quickly to the rigors of the frontier. Her appearance gave the impression of soft Southern daintiness and reserve. But with this she combined unwavering determination and courage. On one occasion, without the slightest concern, she traveled alone with her two sons by covered wagon to an Army outpost in New Mexico. Even her husband lacked her iron will. He found this out when he and Douglas demanded that Douglas be shorn of his girl-like long, curly hair. She did not give her consent until her son was almost five years old.

In those years of continual moving about from one Army

post to another, the chances were slim that the MacArthurs would find a decent school for their two sons. For this reason, Mary MacArthur took it upon herself to direct the education of her boys. Wherever they traveled, her first activity was to convert their quarters to a schoolroom, with lesson books in bookcases and pads of paper, pencils, and maps on table tops.

When he was home from Indian skirmishes (which was not too often), Douglas' father took a hand in educating his boys. From early childhood, he had been a voracious reader. One time he told Douglas that as a youngster he had admired Abraham Lincoln more than any other public figure, and how he had attempted to copy his hero. He would lie on the floor in front of the fireplace and by its light would read, as Lincoln had read, *Robinson Crusoe, Pilgrim's Progress, Aesop's Fables, Life of George Washington,* and the Bible. Even in later years he loved these same books, though he had his nose deep in any others that were shipped to the frontier. In fact, he was so studious that despite his hectic military life, he somehow found time to win a college degree as Doctor of Laws at forty-five, when Douglas was nine years old.

Captain MacArthur was also an excellent speaker. This ability showed up in young Arthur, whose flair for the spoken word was already well-developed in childhood. The elder MacArthur was often called upon to make speeches and he had the knack of bringing a crowd to its feet. However, there was one time when he was unhappy about an invitation to speak. This was at Fort Leavenworth where, said Douglas, "my father came home one night in the greatest possible anger." When Mrs. MacArthur wanted to know what was the matter, he said, "Well, I have just been assigned to make the discussion at next week's Lyceum."

Mrs. MacArthur straightened with pride. "Why, you should be proud of the opportunity. What is the subject?"

"That's just the trouble." Douglas' father smiled weakly. "The subject is: The Spirit of the Age—What Is It?"

Though many found the military life to be a bit like a wandering Arab's existence, almost from the start Douglas was determined on an Army career. The feats of his father in the Civil War never failed to stir his excitement. Also, the quiet bravery of the post soldiers on duty on mountain, desert and prairie frontiers roused his emotions.

Both he and his older brother Arthur practiced marching by the hour, memorized Army regulations and hungrily read military histories and biographies. Douglas was especially impressed with George Washington and Abraham Lincoln and early referred to them as "my advisers." Even before he reached his teens, he was already a superb horseman and rifle shot. A great moment in his life came when he was thirteen. Already tall, dark-haired and strikingly handsome, he possessed the military bearing and posture of a general. Standing within earshot of his parents one day, he heard his father say to his mother, "I think there is the material of a soldier in that boy."

In September of 1893, orders came to the then Major MacArthur to report to Fort Sam Houston at San Antonio, Texas, as assistant adjutant general. Again he and his wife packed their belongings. But this time their son Arthur, Jr., did not accompany them. For the first time the family of four was to be separated.

Douglas' brother, who was three and a half years older than he, had set his sights on an appointment to West Point.

Though his father's Army records credited him with being "beyond question the most distinguished" officer in the Army "for gallantry and good conduct," he lacked the right political connections to help his son. In the end, Arthur had to settle for an appointment to the Naval Academy at Annapolis. This was a blow for Major MacArthur who had visualized both of his sons in the Army uniform of the day.

Mary MacArthur was absolutely determined that Douglas should enter West Point. She inspired him to follow in his father's Army footsteps and told him often he would "be a great man like his father some day." She filled him with ambition, guided his thinking, reading and activities. Though his father had not gone to West Point, it was necessary for Douglas to do so because times had changed and now it was difficult for a non-West Point man to cut his own path in the Army. He must also be an excellent student, for a man who could fight and do nothing else was not the best soldier. Douglas knew well that Army Washington records on his father showed: "Investigations in political economy pursued for many years, through writings of modern economists including Adam Smith, Thomas Robert Malthus, David Ricardo and John Stuart Mill. . . . Special inquiry made into the colonial and revolutionary period. . . . Constitutional development of the Republic. . . . Extensive examination into the civilization and institutions of China."

When the MacArthur trio arrived in San Antonio in the fall of 1893, Mrs. MacArthur was determined that Douglas should enter a military school. The West Texas Military Academy had just come into existence, and she enrolled him. However, she insisted that he attend solely as a day student, for she wanted him home in the evening at the fort where his father's influence would continue. On many evenings, Major MacArthur brought to dinner recent graduates of West Point who would tell Douglas of life there.

Despite his thinness, Douglas proved an excellent athlete at the Academy. He played shortstop on the baseball team and quarterback on the football eleven. "The scrimmages were hard on him," said a classmate. "You could see his lips turn blue but he would get up and fight it again."

However, his mother found more satisfaction in his schoolwork than in his ability on the playing field. He graduated as valedictorian in 1897 with an average of 97.33. Also, as first sergeant of A Company, he led the prize drill squad.

The time had now come to seek an appointment to West Point. Again, as with Arthur, Jr., the right political connections were hard to find. For a while all doors remained closed. Then when hope seemed at an end, a letter came from Congressman Theobald Otjen of Milwaukee, Wisconsin. Otjen wrote that he planned to hold a competitive exam in the spring of the following year to select a West Point candidate and alternate. Elated, Mrs. MacArthur and Douglas hurried to Milwaukee to establish legal residence in the home town of the MacArthurs.

Events now pulled the family apart. In September of 1897 Major MacArthur was promoted to lieutenant colonel and sent to a new post at St. Paul, Minnesota. The following February the battleship Maine blew up in Havana Harbor. A declaration of war against Spain followed on April 7. Shortly afterward, Lieutenant Colonel MacArthur became a brigadier general and was ordered to report to San Francisco "for duty with expedition for Philippines."

He had taken on weight and his step was slower, and his wife was concerned about his fighting in a second major war. However, she did not reveal any of her concern to

Douglas, who had to take his examination only four days after his father was ordered to leave. Her forced smile proved worthwhile, for Douglas came out with a grade of 93.3 per cent, compared with his nearest rival whose score was 77.9.

Nevertheless, there was bad news. The physical examination revealed that he suffered from a spinal ailment. Not to be put off, Mrs. MacArthur took her son to Dr. Franz Pfister, who treated him for a year before he was cured. During the visits, said Dr. Pfister, he and the youth had many conversations. "He was tremendously interested in anatomy, biology, physiology and everything that concerned health and medical science," said the doctor.

During their year's stay at the old Plankington House in Milwaukee, Douglas studied at a local high school, where he took courses in physics and chemistry. He also spent time with his father's relatives, who were struck by the similarity between the two. Though he resembled his mother, he had his father's characteristics, many of which he had consciously acquired. He was extremely neat, as was his father, had the older man's excellent voice, old-world courtesy and modesty. Those who knew Douglas during that year were impressed with his feelings of outrage against injustices then in the news. These ranged from the war with Spain and the fighting in Ethiopia, to the famous Dreyfus trial in France.

The opening at West Point was still available, and in May of 1899, Mary MacArthur had the satisfaction of telling her nineteen-year-old son that the appointment was his. Douglas MacArthur's life work had begun.

Chapter 3

LEADER AT WEST POINT

W<small>HEN</small> Douglas arrived at West Point early in June of 1899, he underwent another physical examination. His fears that his previous ailment might show up under close scrutiny were groundless. The doctors quickly judged his physical condition to be "normal" and gave the following statistics: Height—five feet, ten and one-tenth inches; weight —133 pounds.

Even from the start he stood out among his fellow plebes. A photograph of the 145 first-year men clearly showed Douglas' military heritage. With his backbone like a ramrod, his shoulders squared and his head held high, he was easily distinguishable from the others. Said a fellow classmate, "He had dark hair and a ruddy out-of-doors complexion— a typical Westerner. He was a 'born soldier.'" Nor was he considered a braggart when he flatly announced that he would finish first in his class and would eventually serve as Chief of Staff of the United States Army.

With her husband fighting in the Philippines and Arthur, Jr., at sea as a young naval officer, Mrs. MacArthur decided to live at West Point rather than remain by herself in Milwaukee. She moved into Craney's Hotel, an ancient firetrap where Lafayette had once stayed.

Ulysses S. Grant, III, grandson of President Grant, entered the Academy the same year as Douglas. Like Mrs. MacArthur, his mother moved into Craney's Hotel to be near her son. Malicious gossip in the small town and in the newspapers soon had it that both mothers were in competition with each other through their respective sons, with each supposedly spurring her son on to achieve a better record than the other's. Perhaps there was an element of truth in this. However, the competition was not too keen, for "Doug-y" consistently outdistanced "Lyss-y." Nevertheless, there was no question that a mother who came to West Point with her son was unique. For years afterward gossipmongers and MacArthur detractors called Douglas "the first cadet whose mother went through the Academy with him."

There was little doubt that the presence of his mother and the fact that his father was almost daily in the news coming from the Philippine Islands was a real disadvantage to Douglas. During his plebe year, rough hazing of first-year men by upperclassmen was at its height and special attention was devoted to Douglas. It became commonplace for upperclassmen to order him to stand at rigid attention for an hour. On one occasion, they ordered him to remove all his clothing and do kneebends with arms outstretched in a field of broken glass. Without a protest, he did as he was told, but after a large number of bends his strength sapped and he fell over in a faint.

This did not end the hazing. In the days and weeks that followed, he was ordered to enter scalding steam baths, hang from his tent ropes for minutes at a time and do endless push-ups. Once when he suffered convulsions after a cruel prank, he pleaded with another boy to cover his face with a blanket so no one would hear his outcries.

Another form of hazing was to order the plebes who were sons of soldiers to stand at attention with eyes lowered and recite their father's exploits. Often, just as Douglas was about to eat his first forkful of dinner, this order came. However, he enjoyed talking about his father's military experiences at Kenesaw Mountain, Chicamauga, Missionary Ridge, and atop Lookout Mountain above the clouds during the Civil War. In addition, from letters and newspaper accounts he was fully abreast of his father's activities in the Philippine Islands and treated fellow diners to picturesque recitations of events there.

Douglas was well aware of the senseless cruelty of the hazings. Yet he realized there was no alternative if he hoped to remain at West Point. Several other plebes left the Academy rather than undergo the paddlewhacking, exercising, orders to maintain long periods of silence, and to ignore their closest friends. But Douglas was determined to graduate and he underwent the vicious practices without a whimper.

It was not until he had completed his plebe year that word reached Washington of the severe hazing rituals at the Academy. Angry over these reports, President William McKinley appointed a special committee to investigate. The committee concentrated much of its hearings on Douglas, but he would not involve any upperclassmen. Though he did relate some of the practices he refused to incriminate anyone. However, a fellow tentmate testified on the treatment meted out to Douglas. Asked why Douglas was treated so harshly, the witness said, "MacArthur's real offense was that he was the son of General MacArthur." When asked why Douglas put up with the cruel hazing, the witness replied, "I believe the fact that his mother was at the post led him to put up with more than he otherwise would have done."

During his plebe year, Douglas gained a reputation for serious study and was characterized as having "a mind like a sponge." One advantage he held over fellow plebes was that he roomed with an upperclassman. Those above the plebe level were permitted to keep their lights on for two hours beyond the nine P.M. "lights out" limit for first-year men. Even the eleven P.M. "lights out" call was often too early for Douglas. Some nights he hung a blanket over the window and studied quietly almost until dawn.

When U. S. Grant, III, was also observed studying late, several members of the plebe class under the leadership of Hugh S. "Iron Pants" Johnson of Oklahoma formed the "Salt Creek Club." They were a fun-loving crew, and one of their chief pleasures was sneering at MacArthur and Grant for "extending themselves to come out number one." Douglas' study habits paid off, for he stood first in the plebe class while Grant was second. Only in French did Grant score a higher numerical grade. In Douglas' second year he was again first, but Grant dropped to fourth. However, in his junior year Douglas slipped to fourth in academic standing and Grant to fifth. Then in his final year, Douglas returned once more to first place.

The competition between MacArthur and Grant extended to other areas besides grades. On one occasion, a sculptor traveled to West Point to select a student model for a heroic bronze statue. His fellow cadets were certain that Douglas would be chosen. For as gravel-voiced "Iron Pants" Johnson put it, MacArthur was "the handsomest young man I have ever seen—brilliant and absolutely fearless." The sculptor roamed through the barracks and the fields of the academy and studied each cadet. In the end, he selected Grant as his model, to Mrs. MacArthur's deep disappointment.

Despite his studious habits, Douglas was far from a grind. He was an excellent dancer and was known for his witty comments. According to classmates, somewhere along the line he managed to become engaged to eight girls at the same time, thus breaking the old record of seven. The rumor was that Mrs. MacArthur had a difficult time explaining the situation to all eight girls. Years later, with a twinkle in his eyes, MacArthur said, "I do not remember being so heavily engaged by the enemy."

Douglas also found time for athletics. Each day he put in at least a half hour doing strenuous exercises in the gym. Because he could not gain weight, he did not go out for varsity football, but instead managed the team in his last year. His chief sport at West Point was baseball; he was a regular, playing first base and in the outfield. However, he was not a powerful hitter. He had the distinction of playing in the first baseball game against the rival Naval Academy and scored the first run in the long series. Thus he earned for himself the nickname of "Dauntless Doug." For his baseball prowess, he won the Academy's large "A," which he sewed on a sweater.

With his mother so close by, Douglas spent many of his off-duty hours with her. His first roommate, Arthur Hyde, later recalled, "Every night after supper he spent a half hour with his mother. If he could not get off the grounds, his mother would meet him and they would walk up and down in front of the barracks." He consulted with her on his schoolwork as well as on other matters. For instance, when Hyde first asked him to be his roommate, Douglas told him,

"Would you wait half an hour so I can talk to my mother?" He returned within that time with her approval.

Craney's Hotel was "out of bounds," which meant that any cadet found there was in for severe punishment. On one occasion, Douglas and his later roommate, George Cocheu, disregarded the ruling and visited Mrs. MacArthur at the hotel. They were hardly seated in her parlor when a frenzied bellboy rushed inside with the news that the stern Superintendent of the Academy was on his way to her door for a call.

Mrs. MacArthur quickly determined strategy. There was no back exit from her rooms. Nor was there space for the boys under her bed. The only escape was down a stairway leading to the dark basement. "Go," she ordered them just as the Superintendent rapped on her door.

Tiptoeing into the basement, they could hear her sweet voice as she welcomed her visitor. However, they had just finished congratulating each other, when to their dismay they discovered there was no door leading from the cellar. The only possible escape was through a dust-filled coal chute.

They glanced at their immaculate gray uniforms. Then taking a deep breath, they plunged into the chute. Townsmen saw these blackened figures scurrying toward the barracks. Luckily, they made their way past the guard and got to their room undetected.

Douglas was far from a pious angel at the Academy. Once he raised the reveille cannon to his dormitory roof with the aid of a derrick. Six husky men were required to bring it down again to earth. On an average of ten times a year he was cited on "skin sheets" for infractions of military rules. These ranged from "Long hair at inspection," "Misspelling word in official communication," and "Falling in at formation for inspection without sword" to "In shirt sleeves at inspection" and "Swinging arms excessively marching to front at parade."

However, he did not take part in the serious cadet rebellion against the Superintendent for his harsh rules and regulations. For a while, the cadets subjected the Superintendent to complete silence when he entered the dining hall. When he got even by issuing still harsher regulations, animosity reached a breaking point. One night several of the angry cadets hauled the reveille cannon to the front of the Superintendent's quarters, filled it with rocks and threatened to fire it.

Undaunted, the Superintendent summoned the West Point guard. Unpleasant words were exchanged, but the cadets were dispersed before they could carry out their threat. During the melee, "Iron Pants" Johnson came galloping to the side of MacArthur, who was not a participant. "They are going to charge me with being the ringleader!" he gasped. "I want to be with you so you will be my witness!"

The Superintendent punished all the participants who could be identified. Some suffered immediate discharge from the Academy, others were set back a year. Still others were put under detention. Yet one good result of the rebellion was that the stringent rules were relaxed. To Douglas the entire episode was an important lesson in how not to treat others.

During Douglas' last year at the Academy, the hazing extremes were narrowed considerably. Yet there is no question that had they continued he would not have participated. In fact, even when he had the duty he soon earned the reputation of a "soft touch." For instance, once he chanced upon several cadets playing dice. This was a serious infraction and would have led to severe punishment when reported. While the guilty cadets held their breath and waited, Douglas mumbled something about "seeing spots in front of their eyes" and walked away.

On only one occasion was there any doubt whether he would graduate. During his last year he had trouble with his eyes and was hospitalized. While he lay in bed, he learned that his name had been included in the posted list of "goats," or those who would have to take a special examination in mathematics because they were not doing well. In view of his superior work in math, it irritated him to be classified as a goat simply because he had missed a weekly exam.

Despite efforts by hospital attendants to keep him in bed, he rose, dressed and rushed from the hospital. The home of the head math professor was out of bounds, but he went there regardless and pounded on the door until he was admitted. "I'm going to resign from the Academy if my name is not removed from the goat sheet before classes tomorrow morning," he righteously declared.

In the discussion that followed, the professor made no promises and Douglas finally stalked out. The following morning before classes Douglas was considering how he would explain his resignation to his mother, when a cadet entered his room. "Your name is no longer on the goat sheet," he told him.

At last came graduation day, June 11, 1903. All high honors belonged to Douglas. His four-year scholastic average stood at 98.14, the highest in the Academy's 101-year history. In addition, he held the post of First Captain, the highest student military rank. When Secretary of War Elihu Root handed Douglas his diploma, Mrs. MacArthur saw at last the fulfillment of the first part of her dream.

Chapter 4

FIRST YEARS IN THE ARMY

W<small>HILE</small> Douglas was busy acquiring an education, much had been happening to his father. In July, 1898, three months after the declaration of war against Spain, Brigadier General MacArthur landed in the Philippines. Only a month later he was elevated to Major General because of his role in the capture of Manila. Shortly afterward, Spanish opposition collapsed.

There was great joy in the islands with the defeat of the hated oppressors. However, the question now arose regarding the future of the Philippines. Were the American forces to clear out and turn over the reins of government to local military chieftains? Or was the American Army to remain for a while until order was restored? Under Spanish rule, few Filipinos had been permitted to acquire a college education. With this situation, who would be capable of directing a native government?

President McKinley settled matters by deciding that the Philippine Islands would become an American possession. As he told visiting Methodist missionaries at the White House: "The truth is I didn't want the Philippines when they came to us as a gift from the gods ... but there was nothing left for us to do but to take them all, and to educate the Filipinos and uplift and civilize and Christianize them, and by God's grace to do the very best we could by them."

McKinley's decision came as a great shock to the Philippines. Immediately the natives who had fought so valiantly alongside General MacArthur's men now turned on them in a war for independence. Led by the wily Aguinaldo, they gave no quarter and for the next three years they put up strong resistance. It was not until March, 1901, when one of General MacArthur's aides captured Aguinaldo, that major fighting ceased. Nevertheless, in the tropical hinterland fighting continued several years longer.

During the insurrection, President McKinley had named General MacArthur as Military Governor of the Philippines. Both from his Milwaukee upbringing and from his readings, General MacArthur was a man of democracy. Even while the insurrection was at its bloodiest stage, he had begun the construction of schools, hospitals, and roads. He had also introduced some of the basic civil rights of the American Constitution. His proudest achievement was his instituting the right to the writ of habeas corpus, or the right of a person in custody to be brought before a court to determine whether he is being lawfully held.

In his letters to Douglas and to his wife, General MacArthur expressed the hope that his work in the Philippines would be his crowning achievement. However, this was not to be. In 1900, President McKinley sent William Howard Taft to the islands to establish civil government there. It wasn't long before Taft and MacArthur clashed. MacArthur did not like Taft's reference to Filipinos as "my little brown brothers." In turn, Taft did not agree with General Mac-

Arthur's view that the islands should remain under military rule for several more years. The question soon arose whether the Military Governor or the Civilian Governor would be in charge.

In the end, President McKinley stepped into the middle of this argument. He ruled in favor of civilian control, and in July, 1901, General MacArthur was ordered home.

When Douglas graduated from West Point, his father was stationed in San Francisco. But his exploits in the Philippines had so thrilled his son that Douglas yearned to follow in his father's footsteps. Each year the top ten men of the graduating class were permitted to select their branch of service. Douglas picked the Corps of Engineers where advancements were more rapid. In addition, he requested service in the Philippines.

Shortly afterward the new second lieutenant was on his way to Manila. Hardly had he arrived when he was put to work building barracks, roads and wharves. Later he added to his experience by bossing a surveying crew on Bataan Peninsula in Luzon, near the port of Mariveles.

As he soon learned, danger lurked everywhere, for the insurgents were still active. Once, without provocation, a bolo-swinging Moro charged toward him. MacArthur fired bullet after bullet at the man in self-defense. Yet the Filipino came on until he was almost upon MacArthur before toppling. Examination revealed that all six of MacArthur's shots had penetrated his heart. Shaken by this strange experience, MacArthur nevertheless concluded that if other Philippine warriors were like this opponent they were awesome, brave fighters indeed. In the back of his mind he stored this conclusion for future use.

Another experience revealed that he had a charmed life,

the same as his father. One morning on the Island of Samar, where the insurgents were still active, he was walking along a tropical path with his orderly, when, suddenly, a shot rang out and his orderly fell dead. MacArthur instinctively reached forward to catch the man as he fell. It was lucky that he did, for a second bullet aimed at his heart ripped through the crown of his hat instead. A grizzly sergeant said later, "Now you're living doubly on velvet."

Lieutenant MacArthur remained in the Philippines for a year before he was ordered back to San Francisco to serve in the Golden Gate harbor defenses. Before he sailed, the Manila Promotion Board examined him for advancement to first lieutenant. The officers had served under his father and they delighted in presenting him with a supposedly impossible problem. The stern board chairman asked him how he would defend a harbor with only a few men and little equipment. "Well, MacArthur," he bellowed, "you've just a few hours before the enemy comes over the ridges and the enemy fleet streams in through the mouth of your harbor. What will you do?"

MacArthur answered without hesitation. "There are two things I'd do, sir," he replied. "First, I'd round up all the sign painters in the area and put them to work painting signs that read: 'Beware—This Harbor Is Mined.' Then I'd float these signs out to the mouth of the harbor. After that I'd get down on my hands and knees and pray. Then I'd go out and fight like a tiger."

He won the promotion.

Shortly after Douglas MacArthur returned to the United States, war broke out between Russia and Japan. On a trip to San Francisco, President Theodore Roosevelt had been much impressed with General MacArthur. As a result, he named Douglas' father to serve as military attaché to the American Legation at Tokyo and as chief military observer with the Japanese forces fighting the Russians in Manchuria. The President was concerned about the rising military might of Japan and wanted the best possible military opinion of her strength.

Douglas longed for the opportunity to serve under his father and to watch a war in action. However, his father would not show him any favoritism. It was not until the fighting had ceased that Douglas received word from the War Department that he was to join his father as his aide-de-camp. There followed a joyous nine-month tour of several Asiatic countries where, through his father's mind and eyes, he learned at close range of the rivalries and future war potentialities of the nations there.

This time when Douglas returned to the United States, he was sent for further engineering training to the Engineering School at Fort Belvoir, near Mount Vernon in Virginia. Then because of his handsome appearance, he served as military aide to President Roosevelt during the White House social season. Life was full for him in 1906 when his father was advanced to lieutenant general, making him the senior officer in the entire American Army. This was the rank that George Washington and Ulysses S. Grant had attained before him.

Douglas was certain that his father would next be named as Army Chief of Staff. However, neither he nor his father figured on old animosities taking a hand in this decision. Governor Taft was now back from the Philippines and President Roosevelt had installed him in his Cabinet as Secretary of War. Taft lost little time passing over Lieutenant General MacArthur and awarding the post to one of his former aides. Hurt and embarrassed, the elder MacArthur could not see himself serving at a lesser post. One day he sat down and wrote Taft a long letter, asking for permission to return to Milwaukee to finish writing his Asian report. He would then retire on June 2, 1909. Taft quickly agreed and the career of the old warhorse ended.

Those were unhappy days for Douglas, who felt the hurt in his father's heart. There were many assignments that he believed he should request to further his career. However, he turned his back on all of them and won permission to be assigned to the Engineer Officer at Milwaukee so that he could be near his father.

In Milwaukee, Douglas lived with his parents in a three-story house, to which he returned each evening after a day at the local Army office. These were evenings of long and enthusiastic discussions of military and philosophic matters between the two men. But Douglas was well aware of his father's unremitting sadness, even though the MacArthurs were soon the center of the city's leading social group.

In fact, it was the family's high social position that brought an end to Douglas' stay in Milwaukee. His superior was a Major W. V. Judson, who resented deeply his lieutenant's social standing. Submerged for a while, this animosity broke into the open when the two went on a field trip. The major gave Douglas a tongue-lashing one night when he found that a hotel manager had given Douglas a larger and airier room than he had given the major.

"You got this room because your name is MacArthur!" Judson bellowed.

"I suppose so," Douglas calmly replied.

This only served to make the major more furious. A short time later Douglas received orders to leave Milwaukee and report to Fort Leavenworth. It was a sad farewell that he held with his parents.

With the exception of a short tour of duty in the Panama Canal Zone and a minor stay in Texas, Douglas spent the next four years at Fort Leavenworth where he served as an instructor in advanced engineering. It was here that he met another young lieutenant, George C. Marshall, whom he was to know well in the years ahead.

Douglas was an excellent instructor because he knew his subject thoroughly and could express his ideas with ease. Other instructors, bedeviled by their students' questions after their lectures, were in awe because Douglas did not have this problem. Asked by another instructor for an explanation, he gave it, tongue-in-cheek: "At the end of my first lecture I announce that now is the time for the question period. Then I explain that my father, General MacArthur, used to say there were three types of students who ask questions: the lazy students, the fawning ones who hope to win favor from the instructor by flattering him, and the no-good so-and-sos who want to embarrass the instructor. Then I add quickly, 'Are there any questions?' "

During his stay at Fort Leavenworth, which ended in 1912, Douglas was both a serious student and a jovial after-hours companion. He played on the polo team and was the manager and outfielder on the post baseball team. It was a wonder that he had time for such outside activities, for in 1911, when he was made a captain, he was loaded down with responsibilities. In addition to his teaching, he served as quartermaster, commissary officer, engineer officer and disbursing officer, as well as taking charge of the engineering depot at Fort Leavenworth. Yet he never appeared overburdened or short of temper. Friends during that period recalled how he often wound up an evening singing "Old soldiers never die—they just fade away." However, in September of 1912, this song became a mockery.

For some time he had been concerned with his father's failing health. His mother wrote him that the fiftieth reunion of the 24th Wisconsin Infantry Regiment was scheduled to be held in Milwaukee on September fifth. She didn't want her husband to go, even though he had been asked to speak to his old Civil War comrades.

The day turned out to be the hottest of that summer and Mrs. MacArthur begged the general to stay at home. However, he insisted upon attending and that evening he was seated on the dais when he was introduced to the cheering throng. There were but ninety survivors of the 850 who had marched off with him in 1862, but they made up in noise what they lacked in numbers.

The old general was recalling a humorous adventure that occurred on their march through Georgia—"It was during the campaign of Peach Tree Creek"—when suddenly he mumbled something about not being able to continue and slumped dead in his chair. Overcome with grief, his old adjutant, Captain Edwin B. Parsons, rushed to the platform, yanked an American flag from the wall and covered his dead commander. He stood sobbing a moment, then he, too, suffered a stroke and fell over on the body of the dead general. A few days later Parsons died.

Within two months, the War Department assigned Douglas to the Office of the Chief of Engineers in Washington, D. C. He had asked for this change because his grief-stricken mother was ill and needed care. Army rules prevented her from coming to live with him at Fort Leavenworth, and though the commanding general protested the loss of his outstanding instructor, the War Department permitted Douglas to shift.

Hardly had he settled into his Washington routine when Major General Leonard Wood, the old leader of the Rough Riders and now Army Chief of Staff, took note of him. Quietly, General Wood made inquiries about Captain MacArthur and what he learned pleased him. In November, 1913, he called MacArthur to his office and appointed him a member of the thirty-eight-officer top level General Staff. This was a group that helped the Chief of Staff plan Army policy, and membership in this body was a high honor.

Besides the numerous comments regarding Captain MacArthur's brilliance, there was another MacArthur trait that had led General Wood to appoint him to the General Staff. He always spoke his true mind, regardless of circumstances or consequences. This characteristic revealed itself almost immediately. The General Staff was divided into committees to consider various topics, and before long one-man minority reports signed by MacArthur began to come across Wood's desk. Although the general appreciated this extra view, the minority reports did not sit well with the senior officers on the staff, who considered MacArthur an upstart. Nor was this situation improved when General Staff members learned that General Wood began adopting MacArthur's views. Inevitably, many of the older officers built up resentment against him that lasted throughout their careers.

Nevertheless, Captain MacArthur would not mend his ways in order to be liked. He could well remember the advice his father had given him years before. "Gather all the facts possible and then make your decision on what you think is right as opposed to what you think is wrong. Don't try to guess what others will think, whether they will praise

or deride you. And always remember that at least some
of your decisions will probably be wrong. Do this and you
will always sleep at night."

In 1914, after four years of armed rebellion, the Mexican
revolutionary pot boiled over. In 1912, President Taft ordered Americans to leave this troubled land south of the
border. President Francisco I. Madero was assassinated the
following year and General Victoriano Huerta asserted that
he was now the dictatorial ruler of the country. Huerta's
views were extremely anti-American and President Woodrow
Wilson refused to recognize him. Relations between the
United States and Mexico deteriorated until a low ebb was
reached in April, 1914, when Mexican soldiers at Tampico
insulted the American flag. So great was the outcry in the
United States that President Wilson first ordered the blockade and then the seizure of the port of Veracruz.

MacArthur was eager to see action and he petitioned
General Wood for permission to take part in the expedition
to Veracruz. Reluctant at first, General Wood finally agreed
to send him as an independent agent of the General Staff.
He was not to be part of the regular Army expedition, but
was instead to act alone "to obtain, through reconnaissance
and other means . . . all possible information which would
be of value in connection with possible operations." In other
words, he was to serve as a spy.

As soon as he landed in Mexico, MacArthur learned that
the American Army command was already in full control
of Veracruz. Since April 21, it had dominated the city, yet
it was pinned down as if trapped. The reason for this state
of affairs was obvious. Trains were necessary to bring supplies into the city, yet all Mexican locomotives had mys-

teriously disappeared. To make matters hopeless, American locomotives did not have the same wheel gauge as Mexican locomotives and could not run on Mexican tracks.

In scouting about, MacArthur learned that five Mexican locomotives lay hidden at Alvarado, forty-two miles south of Veracruz. Without informing the Army command, MacArthur made his way stealthily to Alvarado. Here he rounded up some Mexican railroad men who were willing to help him for a payment of $150 in gold to each. He also uncovered the five locomotives, though only three were usable.

After dark that night they began a wild ride back to Veracruz. At Piedra, MacArthur thought it wise to walk around the town and meet the locomotives on the other side. This proved almost fatal, for in passing through town he was attacked by fifteen men on horseback. "I was knocked down by the rush of horsemen," he later noted in his official report, "and had three bullet holes through my clothes, but escaped unscathed." Near Laguna, a bullet went through his shirt "and two others hit the car within six inches of me." But again he remained unharmed.

The firemen stoked the steam engines madly at MacArthur's insistence. But the ancient locomotives could do little more than creep. Finally, just as the sun came over the horizon, the railroad cars chugged safely into American lines.

For this feat, General Wood recommended to the Adjutant General that Captain MacArthur be awarded the Congressional Medal of Honor. Soon after, a board of three officers was selected to consider this recommendation. Its chairman was Colonel Charles G. Treat, a fellow member of the General Staff with MacArthur and Commandant at West Point when MacArthur was a cadet. Colonel Treat reached his decision quickly. MacArthur was not to get the medal.

Chapter 5

OVER THE RAINBOW

Wᴴᴇɴ the United States declared war against Germany on April 6, 1917, Douglas MacArthur was thirty-seven years old and a major. He was then serving as military aide to Secretary of War Newton D. Baker and was in charge of dealing with newspaper reporters for the Department.

For a year before the entrance of the United States into World War I, there was controversy in the Department regarding the composition of our fighting forces. Basically, the argument was whether to expand the National Guard units in the various states into combat divisions or to concentrate on building up the regular Army. For the most part, National Guard units were composed of young men who had regular jobs but who met weekly at armories in their home towns for training and attended encampments at Army forts during their summer vacations. Often, members of the National Guard actually paid for the privilege of military training.

It was Major MacArthur's opinion that the National Guard units be expanded. However, this was a view that was strenuously opposed by encrusted Regular Army officers, who sneered at the ability of voluntary National Guard units to withstand the assault of an enemy's regular army. So far as they were concerned, MacArthur was a traitor to the Regular Army. One one occasion, an officer of superior rank took him aside and said heatedly, "I can see, Major, that you are not interested in pursuing your career much further."

MacArthur made a host of new enemies. However, he was not one to be turned aside by mere threats. With renewed effort he pushed forward his view, both with reporters and Secretary Baker. Just how effective he was with the press was revealed by a letter sent to Secretary Baker that was signed by twenty-nine of the leading Washington correspondents. The closing sentence read: "We cannot but feel that the major has helped, through us, to shape the public mind."

As for Baker, he took MacArthur with him one afternoon to see President Wilson. The issue was thoroughly aired among the three. Impressed with MacArthur's eloquence, the President gave him his blessing.

With the outbreak of war, Secretary Baker wanted to send a trained National Guard division to France immediately to stand alongside British and French allies against the Germans. However, as he wearily pointed out to his aide, he faced a difficult decision. For instance, if he selected the New York National Guard, there would be outcries from New York mothers against sending their sons first. On the other hand, other states might complain that he favored New York.

"There is a way out of your problem, Mr. Secretary," MacArthur told him. "Why don't you form a National Guard division from National Guard units selected from several states? In that way there will be no objections." He swung his arm in a half circle. "It will stretch over the whole country—like a rainbow."

Secretary Baker watched his sweeping arm. "That's what we'll call it," he said excitedly. "The Rainbow Division!"

The Rainbow Division it was called. National Guard units from twenty-seven states came to join it. Its numerical title was the 42nd Division, and Secretary Baker installed aging General William Mann as its commanding officer. "However," said Baker to the general, "I insist that you take Major MacArthur as your chief of staff."

On August 5, 1917, when MacArthur was advanced to infantry colonel, he was already busily at work organizing and training the 42nd Rainbow Division. Noting his enthusiasm and ability, General Mann gave him virtually a free hand. Soon MacArthur had 27,000 men at Camp Mills on Long Island, New York, where they underwent special training. They were a loud and boisterous group, eager to prove their patriotism and fighting worth. They were hard to keep in check because of their excessive energy and enthusiasm. A walk in any direction from the camp's headquarters would immediately bring one face to face with some of the many colorful personalities abounding in the Rainbow Division. Two who were to achieve national fame were William J. "Wild Bill" Donovan and Father Duffy, the renowned chaplain.

In order that the division might go right into action once it reached France, MacArthur painstakingly collected enough gear to last six months. There would be no costly delays on the other side for lack of guns or equipment. Nor could the leaders of the American Expeditionary Forces (A.E.F.) find excuses to keep the Rainbow Division out of the fight.

MacArthur was to learn an important lesson. Collecting gear was important, but so was keeping one's eye on it. By the time the Rainbow Division trod on French soil in December, 1917, most of its supplies had been stolen or ransacked by other outfits. Many of the men lacked winter coats, blankets, and even heavy shoes. This was a shock, but it was to be eclipsed by an even greater blow. Hardly had MacArthur recovered from staring aghast at the condition of the Rainbow's pitiful supply station when he and General Mann were handed an order from staff headquarters of the A.E.F. General John J. "Black Jack" Pershing, head of the A.E.F. Pershing had ruled that the Rainbow Division would not go into battle as a solid division. Instead, its units were to be used merely as replacements for other divisions.

Incensed, MacArthur sent cables back to the War Department in Washington. What was the point of the Rainbow Division if it was not to be a national symbol of the National Guard? Why had its men been permitted to develop teamwork if it was not to be allowed to operate as a unit?

Officers on Pershing's staff were furious when they learned that the leaders of the Rainbow Division had gone over their heads to Washington. How dare MacArthur set himself above General Pershing's orders? How could he, as a member of one outfit, understand the general battle plan?

Pershing, who had a reputation for a quick temper, ordered MacArthur to report to him. He cut through the young colonel as MacArthur refused to alter his position. "Young man," Pershing told him sharply, "I do not like your attitude." Then he ordered MacArthur to leave.

The relationship between the top general and the young colonel did not improve. Shortly after their meeting, the

War Department informed General Pershing that he was not to tamper with the Rainbow Division. The colonel had bested the general, an event that could lead to serious trouble in the colonel's future.

That winter in France was the coldest of the century. The poorly clad men of the Rainbow Division underwent further training for four months. Many of their uniforms had been outmoded even before the Spanish-American War. Some men could not march because their soles had worn out and they had no replacements. However, by dint of hard work, the supply situation gradually improved. Several times orders came transferring the best officers of the Rainbow Division to other outfits. In some instances, MacArthur could do nothing about these raids. However, when the order came to send "Wild Bill" Donovan to another division, MacArthur dropped all caution and interceded directly with General Pershing, who permitted Donovan to remain with the Rainbow Division.

In the spring of 1918, the German objective was to bring the war to a successful finish before the full force of Pershing's two million American soldiers could be moved against her. Unsuccessful in previous attempts to take Paris, the Germans hoped to do so now. That March, the 42nd Rainbow Division moved to the Lunéville-Baccarat sector east of Paris and took its position under experienced French guidance. Battlefields presented a weird sight to the American forces. Stretched out before them was an enormous tangle of barbed wire strung on hastily pounded posts. Large shell craters dotted the scene, and many were filled with muddy stagnant water. The soldier's life was in trenches dug into the ground. Underground behind the trenches were caves on support beams where the men ate and rested

Major General Charles T. Menoher had replaced General Mann as head of the Rainbow Division. Like Mann, Menoher actually turned over the direction of the division to MacArthur. However, he insisted that MacArthur refrain from exposing himself needlessly. Divisional headquarters lay far behind the battleground and he wanted MacArthur to operate from this safe zone.

But this was contrary to MacArthur's nature. Hardly had the Rainbow Division reached Baccarat when he joined a French reconnaissance raid one night into German lines. He made an odd sight in riding breeches, with a riding crop in one hand and a battered officer's cap tilted forward over one eye. The raiders inched their way across no man's land, cutting a path through the jungle of barbed wire. Without mishap they reached the strung German barbed wire and again pliers snipped the sharp wall. A hand grenade went off and the men dived headlong into German trenches on the heads of surprised foes just as the front was raked with machine-gun fire. Hand-to-hand fighting broke out immediately.

After the raid was completed, the French survivors returned to their lines. A tally revealed that MacArthur was not among those present. Just as his name was being crossed from the list of the raiding party survivors, his riding crop was seen in the dull night light. It was MacArthur safely returned and prodding a prisoner before him. However, he looked embarrassed, for he had left the seat of his breeches on the barbed wire in no man's land. For his action, he won his first medal, the Croix de Guerre.

On a second raid, MacArthur won the Distinguished Service Cross. It was fine to show his courage under fire, but this raid almost proved his undoing, for the Germans used poison mustard gas and he was without a gas mask. As a result, he was badly poisoned. Though his adjutant insisted that he be hospitalized, he refused. Almost sightless and quite ill, he nevertheless remained with the division. His sole concession to the worried doctor was to wear a blindfold for ten days to rest his eyes.

The Germans were pounding away at British troops to the north when the Rainbow Division received orders to go over the top. Said MacArthur: "You never know about men until a time like that. You never know what's inside them. I thought I knew what was inside our men, but after all, they were not really professionals. None of them had ever been under fire.

"And then, there we were—ready to go. When the time arrived, I climbed out and started forward. For a dozen terrible seconds, as I went forward, I felt that they weren't following me. But then, without turning around, I knew how wrong I was to doubt even for an instant. In a moment, they were all around me . . . ahead of me."

The Lunéville-Baccarat sector was supposed to be a relatively quiet zone. However, for eighty-two days in a row the Rainbow Division took part in fierce front-line fighting. Machine-gun firing and bursting shells made sleep impossible. During this period the division bore the brunt of the fighting because General De Bazelaire had earlier removed four French divisions of his 7th Army Corps that had been stationed with the Rainbow men. When the fighting ceased on this front, the Rainbow Division was more than battle-scarred, for more than 2,000 of its men were either killed or wounded.

MacArthur's feats were already growing legendary. "The D'Artagnan of the A.E.F." became one of his nicknames.

He would not send his men where he would not go himself. His headquarters were only a thousand yards behind his most advanced trench. Even so, he shared the foul trench existence with the soldiers, crawled through mud with them and exposed himself even more frequently than his men to enemy gunfire.

Back at General Staff headquarters frequent comment was that he was just a showoff. The truth was that he was a colorful individualist no matter what the circumstances. At the front, he wore immaculate riding breeches as if he were going for a canter through the park on a quiet morning. "The Beau Brummell of the 42nd" and "The Fighting Dude" were the nicknames used by his men in referring to his odd war clothing. Often he walked about with a four-yard-long muffler hanging from his neck. This was a gift from his mother to whom he wrote almost daily. He refused to wear the regulation steel helmet or gas mask, nor would he carry a gun. Instead he wore a drooping officer's cap from which he removed the interior wire cap strengthener. In his hand he carried his riding crop. Yet he insisted, and sometimes angrily, that the men wear their steel helmets and gas masks and go about fully armed. He also wore turtle-neck sweaters and often appeared wearing the black West Point sweater with the large "A" he had earned as a baseball player. On his legs he wore mirror-polished riding boots. But this strange attire did not bother his men. "He can chase Germans as well as any doughboy in the Rainbow," said one proudly.

The long eighty-two-day stay on the fighting front turned the weary men of the Rainbow Division into an unkempt lot. None had had a bath during that entire period, and shaving had become a luxury. Sometimes inspectors came from Pershing's headquarters and complained of the grime in the trenches and the lack of cleanliness among the men. Once after listening to a long series of complaints from an inspector, MacArthur shouted at him with fire in his eyes, "If you come back here again, I'll shoot you!" The inspector turned and fled.

On June 21st, when the division was relieved at the front and was heading for a rest in the rear, General Pershing arrived. There was nothing soldierly about the dirty, tired men, and their equipment being loaded on trains at Charmes was mud-caked and battered. Pershing had a reputation for strict discipline. He was aghast at the sight of the men and their equipment. MacArthur expected words of praise from his commanding general. Instead, Pershing turned on him as he stood with his men and yelled, "This division is a disgrace! The whole outfit is just about the worst I have ever seen. MacArthur, I'm going to hold you personally responsible for getting discipline and order into this division!"

MacArthur seethed, but said nothing in justification of the division. Nor had he forgotten this unfair incident five days later when he was notified that he had been elevated to the rank of brigadier general.

On Bastille Day, July 14, 1918, the German army began a new drive. In full fury the Germans attacked Allied lines defended by the one-armed French General Henri Gouraud in the Champagne-Marne area, in a last-ditch attempt to crash through and capture Paris. The Rainbow Division in relief of the 26th Division was then serving under Gouraud and faced the brunt of the attack. Six times in the next six days German divisions assaulted the Rainbow line, and each time they were chased back.

As the sixth attack waned, General MacArthur rode on the running board of an ambulance into the town of Sergy, which had just been captured. His sharp eyes caught the Germans retreating as if they were confused. Hurriedly he raced back to divisional headquarters and confronted his superior, Major General Menoher. "We must attack," he said.

The word "attack" was not in the American military vocabulary in the fighting thus far. Since arriving in France, the Americans had adopted the defensive attitude toward the Germans as practiced by their French and British allies.

"No," Menoher replied. "Besides, every unit is tired out, dead on its feet."

"But we can win a major victory if we go on the offensive," MacArthur argued. Gen. Menoher agreed in the end with MacArthur, though he would not put his oral approval in writing.

MacArthur raced back to the exhausted men of the Rainbow Division. He hurried up and down the line, patting backs, offering encouragement and telling the men about his proposed offensive. In groups, the tired men straggled to their feet, shook off their bone-soaked weariness, and, aroused, they followed him. Picking up their second wind as they moved forward, they chased the Germans across the Ourcq River. Though they were soaked from wading across the stream, they continued the pursuit.

General Peyton C. Marsh, soon to be Army Chief of Staff, commented: "They engaged and used up six enemy divisions." In writing up MacArthur's venture, General Menoher stated: "He organized the entire division into prompt pursuit which soon brought him on the very heels of the enemy and gained entire possession of the great massif of the Forêt de Nesselers, sparing a fresh division from the labors of penetration of this large territory and leaving its full force available for a running relief at the end to deliver the entire weight of its blow."

For this show of offensive ability MacArthur won another decoration. Even more important to him, General Menoher agreed to let him take over the personal command of the 84th Infantry Brigade of the Rainbow Division.

By September, the Rainbow Division was on the St. Mihiel front. This was the first operation by an army composed solely of American divisions. For four years now the Germans had held a triangular area twenty-five miles long and fifteen miles deep that extended into territory held by the French. This area was vital to the Germans because it served their road and rail communications center in the city of Metz. If they lost Metz, the Germans would have to retreat and all their positions westward toward Paris would be endangered. Marshal Ferdinand Foch, the Allied commander, had told General Pershing that his divisions should not go beyond winning the triangle and pushing the Germans back to the Hindenburg Line at the base of the triangle. It was Foch's position that the Americans were too inexperienced to go beyond this goal.

On September 12, the great American offense against the head of the triangle began. For eight days the battle went on to dislodge the Germans. During all this time, MacArthur's men swore that they never saw him sleep. He was everywhere encouraging his men, his absurdly long scarf flapping in the breeze. MacArthur's brigade moved like lightning, ranging far ahead of the American lines. Time after time he had to send orders back to his brigade headquarters to move forward quickly in order not to lose contact with him. One order read: "Pack up completely, trucks, motorcars and motorcycles with all maximum speed possible to

Essey, where I will have somebody there to meet them. I myself will probably have moved forward to Pannes."

During this period other characteristics of MacArthur became clear to his men. One was his belief that he would never be killed in battle. Once when he was seated at a table with his staff at headquarters an orderly came into the room with a tray of food. A shell exploded and the orderly was blown to bits. The staff members hurriedly made for the exits and were almost outside when MacArthur called them back. "Sit down again with me, gentlemen," he told them. "You'll be safe because the Germans can't make a shell to kill me."

Another characteristic was his premonition of impending trouble. During the St. Mihiel offensive, he had made his temporary headquarters in the 100-room Château Saint-Benoît, the former German headquarters. One night he grew noticeably edgy and told his staff suddenly, "We'd better get out of here." They looked at him, puzzled, but obeyed. MacArthur led them to a forest where he proceeded to bed himself down for the night. They were hardly there when an enormous German barrage of shells completely destroyed the château.

MacArthur was slightly wounded during the St. Mihiel fighting, but he did not even pause to clean his wound at a field station. He was on the move and he smelled an important American breakthrough. In his race forward, prodding his brigade, he came to a point where he could see the fortress city of Metz in the distance. There seemed to be little standing in the way of the city's capture. He realized that if he achieved this the German army at the front lines would be bottled up and the war could be quickly brought to an end. He paused only momentarily to study

the outlines of Metz and rushed to Pershing's headquarters
for permission to attempt to take the city.

An infantry captain told of MacArthur's meeting with
General Pershing. " 'Black Jack' Pershing practically threw
him out of his headquarters yesterday. MacArthur came
busting in hot from the front to tell the Old Man that his
84th Brigade had broken through the German lines and that
there was no organized resistance ahead of him. He insisted
that the so-called Hindenburg Line was merely staked out
in that area. The Germans hadn't had time to dig in. He
wanted to be turned loose, no matter what Foch had said.
They say he said to Pershing, 'Let me go and I'll be in Metz
in forty-eight hours. Then you'll make me a major general
and the President will make you a field marshal.' Black Jack
chased him out, but I'll bet he wished he hadn't agreed to
halt the advance as soon as the Heinies had been pushed out
of the St. Mihiel salient. This MacArthur is a cocky guy, all
right, but he sure is a fighting general."

Pershing could not go back on his promise to Foch, and
Metz remained in German hands.

On October 1st, the Rainbow Division moved to the
Meuse-Argonne sector, where more than one million American soldiers of twenty-seven divisions were engaged in this
drive. Word from headquarters was that the final objective
was the city of Sedan. If this city could be captured, the
vital last-ditch German defense line, or the so-called Hindenburg Line, would be smashed and the war might be brought
to a swift conclusion.

On the maps this looked like a fairly simple operation. But
the harsh truth was that the hills and woods along the way
were solidly defended by German machine gunners and

cannoneers. Moreover, this was the rainy season and the roads were muddy ruts and dangerously slippery.

In addition, as MacArthur was soon to discover, the desperate Germans were again using poison gas. This burst in the American lines and hovered in the atmosphere over large areas. Without a gas mask, MacArthur was once more a victim of the poison gas. He also suffered his second wound, but as before, he refused to be hospitalized. Thin and ill, he insisted upon staying with his men.

One night while MacArthur was eating dinner, General Charles P. Summerall, in charge of the American Fifth Army, came to him through the driving rain. MacArthur was wearing his battered cap and West Point sweater, and his long scarf was twined around his neck. As the two sat drinking coffee, Summerall ordered him to attack the heavily fortified Côte de Châtillon, a key hill in the Hindenburg Line that held up the American advance for several days. "You will give me Côte de Châtillon tomorrow or turn in a report of five thousand casualties," Summerall said tensely.

MacArthur did not agree with Summerall's order for a frontal attack on the hill. Up that whole side stretched miles of barbed wire and large numbers of machine-gun nests. A frontal attack would only result in a needless slaughter of his men. He argued instead for a surprise night bayonet attack, and when General Summerall agreed, MacArthur said, "This brigade will capture Côte de Châtillon, sir, or you can report every man in it a casualty. And at the top of the list you will find the name of the brigade's commander."

MacArthur ordered his staff to plan the bayonet assault on the hill. However, in the back of his mind there lurked the notion that a better method might be found. When the rain ended, he quickly ordered that an aerial reconnaissance map be made of the hill and its approaches. A few hours later the map was in his hands and he studied it carefully. Suddenly a smile crossed his face. The map clearly revealed that a gap existed in the barbed-wire defenses on one flank. The men might easily slip through here and take the Germans by surprise.

That night, after a prolonged American barrage, MacArthur led his men through the barbed-wire gap and captured Côte de Châtillon with few casualties.

Shortly afterward, General Menoher, who commanded the Rainbow Division, left that command and was elevated to head the American Sixth Army Corps. MacArthur was advanced to commander of the entire Rainbow Division, which he had run in fact if not in name. Before Menoher departed, he wrote to General Pershing: "I do not feel that I am free to assume another command without recording the services rendered by General Douglas MacArthur, throughout the period during which I commanded the 42nd Division. These services have been so soundly, brilliantly and loyally performed.

"He has stood for the actual physical command of large bodies of troops in battle, not a day but of days' duration. I believe he has actually commanded larger bodies of troops on the battle line than any other officer in our Army, with, in each instance, conspicuous success."

By November 1, 1918, the war was rapidly coming to a close. The Germans were now in full retreat and the American forces drove near Sedan. The French had expressed their desire to be first into the city because it was the scene of their greatest defeat in the Franco-Prussian War of 1870. However, General Pershing's headquarters issued an order that the American 1st Division was to be accorded this privilege.

Unfortunately, the order created great confusion among the divisions driving on Sedan. Previously each division was given a corridor of certain width in which to operate. In this manner, the various divisions would stay out of each other's path. However, the last sentence of Pershing's order said that the boundaries were to be ignored.

As a result, on the night of November 5th, the 1st, 2nd, 6th, 31st, and 42nd Rainbow divisions crossed into each other's territory in the darkness and were soon a directionless mob.

It was during this wild night that the 1st Division "captured" MacArthur. He had set out with his chief of staff on a personal reconnaissance to straighten out the trouble, for he realized that if the Germans knew what was occurring they could have slaughtered thousands of Americans. In the early morning MacArthur suddenly heard guns being cocked. He turned quickly and found himself staring into the muzzle of guns held by a patrol of the 1st Division. Despite MacArthur's protests that he was an American general, the young lieutenant in charge of the patrol arrested him as a German spy. MacArthur's sloppy cap and nonregulation clothing were convincing proof to him that MacArthur was not in the American Army. He marched MacArthur back at gunpoint until a Rainbow Division patrol approached and identified their leader. Later the lieutenant declared that his first impulse had been to shoot MacArthur, but he had not because he thought the "spy" would be more valuable alive than dead.

In the meantime, the French slipped into Sedan and were the first to occupy the city.

After the Armistice on November 11th, MacArthur and the Rainbow Division entered Germany as part of the

Army of Occupation. The Division was in charge of the area from south of Bonn to Koblenz, linked with the British in the north at Cologne and with the French to the south at Frankfurt. MacArthur had no taste for such duty because he believed then that military occupation only served to bring on new animosities among occupied peoples and laid the groundwork for future wars.

He was, therefore, glad in April, 1919, when the Rainbow Division left Europe for home, although he was sorry that the division would no longer be in existence. He had memories enough to last a lifetime. He was thirty-nine now and a national hero, even though the recommendation that he be awarded a Congressional Medal of Honor was not approved. Secretary of War Newton D. Baker publicly hailed him as "our greatest front-line Commander." But he hardly looked the part on his return voyage home as he paced the decks of the ship in a raccoon coat and his long scarf.

Chapter 6

RETURN TO WEST POINT

$\mathbf{W}$HEN Brigadier General MacArthur stepped off the ship from Europe, he wondered what would lie in store for him. After the wartime experiences he had gone through, life on an Army post would be tame in comparison.

He did not have long to ponder his immediate future. Arriving in Washington, D. C., he received word that General Peyton C. March, Army Chief of Staff, wanted to see him. March had served as an aide to MacArthur's father in the Philippines and he well remembered how the elder MacArthur had once confided to him, "I started Douglas for West Point the day he was born."

MacArthur had hardly sat down in the chair facing General March when the Chief of Staff said abruptly, "I want you to take over as Superintendent of West Point."

MacArthur was thrilled at this opportunity to return to the school he had left sixteen years before, in 1903. "But there are lots of problems." General March put a damper on MacArthur's happy expression. "The Academy is forty years behind the times."

He went on to say that almost 9,000 officers had been killed or wounded in France. The country was badly in need of creating a whole new officers' corps. It would be MacArthur's responsibility to lay the groundwork for this endeavor. He would have to set new standards, modernize the institution, and take the lead in combating opposition from those who considered West Point a waste of money.

General March turned to immediate problems. The old West Point, as MacArthur remembered it, no longer existed. The Academy had fallen on evil days. The chief culprit was the war in Europe. During the war, General Pershing had called insistently for more and more officers. The Academy had cooperated by shortening its four-year course in order to speed officers to him. But the result was that cadets at West Point were commissioned with as little as a year of training at the Academy. In their wake, the old traditions were gone, including the celebrated honor system. In addition, the academic coursework had not been changed in decades and barely took into account the tremendous advances made in many fields during the twentieth century.

"So you see what you will be up against," said General March.

General MacArthur's mother had spent the war period at the San Diego naval base with the family of her older son Arthur. Douglas wrote to her now, and early in June mother and son moved into the Superintendent's residence at the Academy on the Hudson.

General March had not overstated the problems at the Academy. "When I assumed command on June 12, 1919," MacArthur later reported to the War Department, "I found there two classes in the Academy, each of them under instruction less than a year. . . . The morale of the cadet body was low. Following the Armistice, 24 cadets resigned from the Fourth Class A and 85 from the Fourth Class B. The academic qualifications for admission had been largely discarded in the case of cadets who entered in November, 1918, and 73 failed in the spring tests.

"The traditional disciplinary system, so largely built around the prestige and influence of the upperclassmen, was impossible in a situation where there were no upperclassmen. Cadet officers had never known the example of cadet officers before them. . . . The old West Point could not have been recognized in the institution as it appeared in June, 1919. It had gone; it had to be replaced."

One of the first tasks MacArthur set upon himself was the modernization of coursework. But here he ran into the almost solid opposition of the faculty. So far as the instructors and professors were concerned he was poking about in an area where he was entirely ignorant. They looked away when he said that the future West Point officer must be a "type possessing all the cardinal military virtues as of yore but possessing an intimate understanding of the mechanics of human nature, a comprehensive grasp of world and national affairs."

For several weeks, he listened to them and watched them shake their heads at each of his suggestions. Finally, one day when a colonel-professor rose to his feet and objected to one of his proposals, MacArthur decided he had had enough. "Sit down, sir!" he shouted. "I have the floor." He turned on the colonel and scolded him for fifteen minutes.

After that he decided that the Academy would modernize its military courses, teach twentieth-century science, add courses in political science and economics, and place greater emphasis on history courses. At great length he outlined what he expected from the English Department, for as he said, "I regard it as the most important department. Without it a man may have the finest judgment in the world, he may even be wise as Solomon, and yet his influence will be practically negligible. . . . The pen is still mightier than the sword."

Even though his funds were limited, he brought in new teachers from other colleges. Several had outstanding reputations in their fields and he constantly prodded them to demand more and more from their students. The older faculty members continued to object, but MacArthur used every means possible to thwart them. On one occasion when several of them requested a meeting with him, MacArthur's adjutant asked, "Shall I call them to meet at eleven o'clock?"

"No!" answered MacArthur. "Call the meeting at four-thirty in the afternoon. I want them to come here hungry— and I'll keep them here until I get what I want."

MacArthur also reinstalled the honor system under which each cadet was to follow a prescribed code of high individual conduct. "West Point men," he said, "have to be clean, live clean and think clean." It was his conviction that if a man in civilian life were untruthful or dishonest, the penalties might be the loss of friends or lawsuits. But if a soldier had these faults he would affect the lives of others and harm his country's honor.

He was extremely stern when it came to violations of the code of honor. When one of the cadets violated the code, MacArthur immediately dismissed him from the Academy. Pressure came from the War Department in Washington to reinstate the young man. However, MacArthur refused. "That man committed an offense against the honor of the

Corps," he said. "He shall never return to the Academy so long as I am its Superintendent!"

Another time, a cadet who was disliked generally underwent harsh hazing. As a result, he later reported to the commandant that this hazing was affecting his studies. Because of his complaint the other cadets considered him a "squealer." One night some of the cadets hustled him to a railroad station, forced him on a train and warned him never to return to West Point. When MacArthur heard about this incident, he ordered the Cadet First Captain removed from that position, even though this cadet had been unaware of the escapade. No amount of pleading by others made him alter his decision. "When I was First Captain," he said, "if this had occurred, I would have considered myself responsible."

At the same time that MacArthur severely enforced the code of honor, he eased the life of the cadets. He abolished all hazing. He also saw to it that the cadets were treated like adults and not children. He passed a ruling that cadets with good grades could get weekend leave. He also gave the men spending money, so that those who came from poor families would not feel socially inferior.

It was MacArthur's idea that every man at West Point must participate in sports. "Nothing more quickly than competitive athletics," he said, "brings out the qualities of leadership, quickness of decision, promptness of action, mental and muscular co-ordination, aggressiveness and courage." Since all the men were not capable of making the regular football, baseball or basketball squads that competed with other colleges, MacArthur set up an enormous intramural program that took in every man and covered almost every known sport. This program proved a tremendous success from the start. In the gymnasium he hung a plaque with his words:

> Upon the fields of friendly strife
> Are sown the seeds
> That, upon other fields, on other days,
> Will bear the fruits of victory.

MacArthur also insisted that the officers and faculty at the Academy take part in athletics. A few showed remarkable ability in competition. Once when he presented a silver loving cup to Chaplain Clayton "Buck" Wheat for winning a skeet-shooting contest against Captain Omar Bradley and other competitors, he jokingly told the chaplain, "Sometime this fall I presented you with a cup as the champion golfer in the Officer Corps here at the Point. A little later I had the honor of handing you the championship cup as the best tennis player among the officers here at the Academy. And today I am presenting you this silver cup for being the finest skeet shooter at West Point. But in all sincerity I must warn you that when you presume to win against the Army in a matter of shooting, which is its peculiar field, then, sir, you have gone just a little too far."

MacArthur maintained a daily schedule that did not meet with the approval of various faculty members, who believed he was not setting a good example for the cadets. However, his schedule was one that suited him perfectly. Colonel Louis E. Hibbs, his adjutant, said, "His custom was to come to his office at eleven A.M. The purpose behind this was to give his entire staff enough time to get everything in order without the pressure of his being present. Upon his arrival he would finish his mail in less than an hour. The hour from 12 to 1 P.M. was given over to interviews. He went to his home from 1 to 3 P.M. where his mother kept house for him. Returning at three, he held official meetings and left between 4:30 and 5 P.M.

"During this daily routine he accomplished a tremendous amount of work. He preferred to meet his officers face to face, and disliked the old method of typewritten sheets being shifted from office to office. He never let any work that came in one day hang over until the next."

While MacArthur was devoting his energies to saving and modernizing West Point, he was not without his problems. In January, 1920, his temporary wartime rank as brigadier general was made permanent by Secretary of War Baker. Most of the other officers who had attained temporary wartime rank of general were, on the other hand, reduced in grade to major and colonel. The result was a great deal of grumbling about MacArthur. A growing number of resentful officers took to calling him the "kid general." "When you become a general, Louie," he told Colonel Hibbs, his adjutant, "you haven't any friends."

Another difficulty he faced was of more significance. With the war over, a vast antimilitary feeling swept the country. Speakers declared that the recent war was the world's last war. Demands rose to eliminate the Army entirely. In Congress, military budgets were slashed to the bone.

It was MacArthur's job to come to congressional committees and plead the case for not only maintaining West Point but for strengthening the Academy. On all sides he underwent attack for his demands. "I am a soldier, not a political engineer," he said. "A comparatively small outlay by the United States will serve in the future to lessen the tremendous expense and the loss of blood for which no money can repay when the unforeseen tragedy is upon us." His eloquence showed him to be a first-rate politician, for without him the Academy might have gone down the drain.

In 1922, when MacArthur was forty-two years old, an important change took place in his life. The year before, when Warren Harding succeeded Woodrow Wilson as President, General Pershing became Army Chief of Staff. Almost everyone in Washington understood that Pershing intended to marry Mrs. Henrietta Louise Cromwell Brooks, a wealthy and charming young woman who acted as his official hostess. Mrs. Brooks had earlier been divorced and was the mother of two children. Then one evening the cadets held a ball at West Point and Mrs. Brooks came. General MacArthur danced with her, and before the ball was over she agreed to marry him.

Generally, the Superintendent of West Point held that post for four years. MacArthur had been there almost three years when he was married on February 14, 1922. Shortly afterward word came from Washington that he was being reassigned to the Philippines. Asked by reporters whether MacArthur's marriage had anything to do with this shift, General Pershing replied, "It's all poppycock, without the slightest foundation and based on the idlest gossip."

MacArthur would have enjoyed remaining at the Academy to complete the job he had begun. But he knew that he had set a fresh course for West Point and he had no regret over his assignment to the Philippines, which he had not visited for almost twenty years.

The Philippine tour of duty lasted until 1925 and left him with mixed feelings. His bride disliked the heat that blazed almost like a furnace. She also found Manila dull, and in 1924, despite her wealth, she became a part-time Manila policewoman to keep herself busy. MacArthur was not interested in parties, dancing or social calls, but preferred to spend his time on military duties and studies. By now he was fully convinced that the Japanese would attempt to become master of Asia. Once, riding in a boat around the Bataan Peninsula, he said to the astonished captain, "Some day the Japanese will attack the Philippines. And if I'm here, I'll make them fight it out on Bataan." Later he made a complete survey of Bataan Peninsula and drew up a defense plan.

He was faced with many irksome matters during the stay. The islands contained many officers who belonged to the substantial group who disliked him because they were either jealous of him or thought he had got ahead too fast. He found that they would not accept him. In addition, he was given humiliating minor assignments that a young lieutenant should have handled. But he never complained.

Then there were family troubles. Mrs. MacArthur's small daughter came down with a serious case of malaria. A cable arrived from Washington in February, 1923, saying that Douglas' mother lay on her deathbed. He hurried back to the United States, fully expecting he would be too late to see her alive. Her doctors gave him small hope that she would live, but the sight of her son gave strength to her weak heart and she recovered. Then that December, when he was back in Manila, there came another cable. He was certain that this time his mother was dead. With trembling hands he read the message and he sat stunned for a long time. His brother Arthur, a forty-seven-year-old Navy captain with a superb record, had died of appendicitis.

Early in 1925, MacArthur received word that he was being promoted to major general (the youngest in the Army), and that his Philippine tour of duty was at an end. He came home to take command of the 4th Army Corps area at Atlanta and a few months later he became commanding general of the 3rd Corps in Baltimore.

Hardly was he in Baltimore when he was thrust into one of the most distasteful tasks of his career. Since the end of World War I, Brigadier General William "Billy" Mitchell had fought for a separate and modern air force. He had traveled the country making speeches and writing newspaper and magazine articles on this subject. Army and Navy officers who scoffed at the war potential of the airplane found him a menace to their old-fashioned position. In September, 1925, when a rickety Navy seaplane crashed on a flight to Hawaii, Mitchell blamed the loss on the "almost treasonable administration of the national defense by the War and Navy Departments." This statement brought fury to the military departments. Charged with insubordination, he was relieved of his duty and ordered to Washington for court-martial.

It was MacArthur's ill fortune to be ordered to serve on the twelve-man court-martial board for the widely publicized trial that lasted from October 28 to December 17, 1925. Billy Mitchell's father had served alongside Douglas MacArthur's father in the Civil War. As a young lieutenant, Billy himself had served under General Arthur MacArthur in the Philippines. Both families hailed from Milwaukee, and when as a child Douglas went there on visits with his mother, he had played with Billy. The family friendship was resumed when General MacArthur retired from the Army and Douglas served in Milwaukee. At one time Milwaukee society buzzed with gossip that Douglas planned to marry one of the Mitchell girls. In fact, he had written the following poem to one of Billy's sisters:

Fair Western girl with life awhirl
Of love and fancy free,
'Tis thee I love
All things above
Why wilt thou not love me?

During the seven weeks of Billy Mitchell's trial, Douglas MacArthur did not utter a single word. Yet there were indications of his regard for Billy. At one point when Billy Mitchell entered the courtroom he greeted MacArthur and shook his hand. The wives of both men also came together to the courtroom each day of the trial.

When the vote came on December 17, Mitchell was found guilty. He was sentenced to suspension from duty and pay for five years. The following February he resigned from the service.

For years afterward reporters asked MacArthur how he had voted. When he maintained stony silence, it was assumed that he had voted against his friend. As the years went by, officers who belonged to the group of MacArthur detractors openly declared that he had voted against Mitchell, thus exposing himself as untrue to Mitchell and also as opposed to progress in military aviation. It was not until a quarter of a century later that General MacArthur informed Senator Alexander Wiley of Wisconsin that he had voted "not guilty." He wrote the Senator, "Mitchell never ceased to express his gratitude for my attitude."

Chapter 7

ARMY CHIEF OF STAFF

Following the trial of Billy Mitchell, General Mac-Arthur returned to his command over the 3rd Corps area at Baltimore. Here as at West Point, he insisted that the soldiers take part in a strenuous athletic program in addition to their regular military training. Visiting generals found the air in MacArthur's camps filled with footballs, baseballs, basketballs and tennis balls. So successful was his athletic program that he was selected to serve as president of the American Olympic Committee for the Olympic Games to be held at Amsterdam, Holland, in the summer of 1928.

It was not long before all the athletes under his command found that he was determined to win the international competition. "We did not come here to lose gracefully," he said, as if he were in the midst of a battle. In the first boxing match between an American and a youth from South Africa, the judges unfairly awarded the decision to the South African. When the boxing manager of the American squad angrily announced he would withdraw his other boxers, MacArthur cornered him and bellowed, "Just remember, sir, Americans do not quit!" The team remained in competition.

In the 400-meter event, Ray Barbuti of Syracuse University was the winner. MacArthur congratulated the panting, tired athlete, then said casually, "By the way, Ray, I want you to run the anchor leg on the 1,600-meter relay."

Barbuti protested that he was winded. Besides, the American relay team did not include him.

"You must do it for your country," MacArthur insisted.

Barbuti ran a brilliant race as anchor man and brought in the baton before anyone else.

In his report to President Calvin Coolidge, MacArthur wrote poetically about "that indomitable will for victory which marked the deathless rush of Barbuti; that sparkling combination of speed and grace by Elizabeth Robinson which might have rivaled even Artemis herself on the heights of Olympus. . . . Nothing has been more characteristic of the American people than their genius for athletics."

Immediately upon his return with the Olympic squadron, MacArthur was ordered to proceed to Manila to command the Department of the Philippines. His wife refused to return there with him. In fact, her wealthy family had offered him several business opportunities if he would leave the service. However, MacArthur pushed aside all such offers. The result was that he proceeded to Manila alone, and a short time later his wife divorced him.

This time in Manila he became quite friendly with Manuel Quezon, who had surrendered to his father in 1901. Quezon was now President of the Philippine Senate, and destined to become first President when his country gained her independence from the United States. One characteristic of Mac-Arthur's that endeared him to Quezon was that he did not discriminate against Filipinos. For example, MacArthur found that the previous American commander had ordered enlisted Filipinos to ride on the bottom deck of military vessels. "Change that at once," MacArthur said curtly to an aide when he learned of it.

MacArthur also became a friend to Sergio Osmena and Manuel Roxas, both destined for important roles in their nation's history. With Governor General Henry L. Stimson, he worked in close harmony in establishing the first defense program for the islands. The Japanese militarists had already begun bombing Manchuria and Stimson feared for the future of the Philippines.

In 1930, MacArthur made a major step forward in his career. That year the Army was to get a new Chief of Staff. Although General Pershing had retired, he still wielded an enormous amount of authority. It was his opinion that one of his two former aides should rise to this post. However, Secretary of War Patrick J. Hurley, who had served under Pershing in the European fighting of 1917-1918, favored MacArthur.

Finally, President Herbert Hoover called in the two men to argue out the matter. Pershing strenuously promoted his suggested appointees. Just as strenuously, Hurley recited MacArthur's many accomplishments. Finally General Pershing dropped his opposition. "Well, Mr. President," he addressed Hoover, "Pat Hurley was one of my boys in France. Let him go ahead and make his own mistakes."

MacArthur proved to be far from a mistake when he donned the four stars of a full general and became Chief of Staff in November of 1930. Bursting with pride, his mother, now seventy-seven, moved into the Chief of Staff's headquarters at Fort Myer and became his hostess and closest associate. Seldom did he go out, but came home instead to discuss his problems and the day's activities with his mother.

This was not a period of complete pleasure, even though he held the post his father had once coveted and failed to gain. MacArthur soon found that the size of the Army he had inherited was below the point of national safety. There were only 12,000 officers and 125,000 men. Of these, fewer than half were actually engaged in the duties of field soldiers. Yet a pacifist and budget-minded Congress wanted even this total decreased. Few agreed with him when he argued that "an adequate army is to the nation as an adequate fire department is to the city."

Disillusionment had set in among Americans regarding the purposes of World War I. Talk was common that the United States should never have entered that war; that in the future Americans should not involve themselves in the affairs of other nations; that the oceans protected the United States from any foreign attacks. MacArthur could not convince others that this was all poppycock. In Asia, the Japanese were already on the march. In Europe, Adolph Hitler's Nazi followers were rising to power with their demands for world conquest. It was to the advantage of aggressors to have a weak United States.

In 1931, MacArthur traveled to Europe to study at first hand the growth of the new militarism. What he saw only served to increase his concern over his country's lack of adequate military strength. While he was abroad, President Hoover cabled him to attend the League of Nation's Disarmament Conference. MacArthur bluntly refused and wired back to the White House, "The way to end war is to outlaw war, not to disarm."

In the United States, General MacArthur soon gained the reputation of a warmonger. Not only did he want to increase the size of the Army but he also wanted more dreadful weapons. "Armies and navies give weight to the peaceful words of statesmen," he said, "only when they are known to be efficient." He also went on to argue that "it has been said that had there been a Regular Army of 20,000 men at Bull Run, the Civil War never would have been fought."

Despite great opposition to his demands for adequate defense, MacArthur would not give up his fight. One of his first struggles as Army Chief of Staff was to prevent Congress from cutting two thousand officers off the measly twelve thousand total. This turned into a seven-months' arguing session before congressional committees. He insisted: "An army can live on short rations, it can be insufficiently clothed and housed, it can even be poorly armed and equipped. But in action it is doomed to destruction without the trained and adequate leadership of officers." MacArthur won this fight, though Congress slashed the Regular Army budget by 38 per cent over a two-year period.

Congress knew him as a man who would not give up, no matter how great his disappointment. "I have humiliated myself," he admitted to a congressional committee. "I have almost licked the boots of some gentlemen to get funds for the motorization and mechanization of the Army." One Congressman called him "a thief"; another "a polished popinjay." MacArthur took all these insults until one day when he felt he could take no more. His eyes flashed and he pushed his chair back in the congressional committee room as he angrily rose to his feet. "Gentlemen, you have insulted me," he lectured the members. "I in my profession am as high as you in your profession. When you are ready to apologize, I shall return!" With that, he walked from the room. Members later apologized.

Despite his severely limited budget, MacArthur brought

many important innovations into the American Army. "Tanks—planes—submarines will be the decisive weapons in the next war," he said flatly. "Mass movements of airplanes and huge concentrations of tanks will win the battles." He proposed using the Garand rifle, greater air power, armored tanks, mobility in the field for daring striking power, a self-written plan for industrial mobilization in case of war, and a Selective Service plan. Some opponents claimed that these were unnecessary. Years later still other opponents said that he had been too cautious and did not do enough. So far as the soldiers under him were concerned, his leading achievement came when he dropped the rigid and uncomfortable old uniform and permitted a new uniform with its soft collar and open jacket.

Fortunately, General MacArthur had the support of Secretary of War Hurley in his fight for an adequate defense program. Frequently when Hurley dropped into his office, MacArthur would be pacing the floor and wearing a long Japanese gown as he dictated speeches and programs. "Thank God, the General is right most of the time," said Hurley. "It's almost impossible to convince him of it when he's wrong. Takes all night and all the next day and sometimes a month or two."

In the summer of 1932 there occurred what MacArthur called "the most distasteful duty" of his entire career. The great economic depression had blanketed the nation and more than 15,000,000 persons were without jobs. That spring, about 20,000 unemployed World War veterans and wives and children came to Washington to beg Congress for a money bonus for service in that war. They built shacks near the Capitol and for two months the Bonus Army roamed the lobbies and pleaded with congressmen. When Congress did not act in their behalf, many grew bitter. Some Communists in the midst of these bedraggled souls tried to lead them to riot.

The presence of the Bonus Army created a serious situation, even though one could be only sympathetic with these poor people. In any event, the government made no effort to handle the problem until it was too late. When they had first walked into Washington, MacArthur set up Army kitchens for them, but he was soon ordered to discontinue them. He also passed out money to Rainbow Division veterans.

Then on July 28, 1932, President Hoover ordered Secretary Hurley to drive the Bonus Army squatters out of town. Hurley passed the order on to MacArthur. In turn, the General could have passed the order on to an underling, such as his personal aide, Major Dwight D. Eisenhower. Instead, he said, "I would not give this distasteful job to any other officer. If anything went wrong, it would be the kiss of death for his future."

When the order came, MacArthur was wearing a white summer suit. He had no uniform in his office and called home to have one sent to him. What arrived was one whose jacket was covered with medals. With his aide, Major Eisenhower, he then rode out on horseback to direct the Army tanks and cavalry, under Major George S. Patton, in the task of ridding Washington of the Bonus Army.

MacArthur ordered his soldiers not to fire any bullets at the veterans. Their weapon was to be tear-gas bombs. Not long after the army tanks began rumbling down Pennsylvania Avenue, MacArthur himself was one of the first victims of the tear gas. The shacks were burned and the Bonus Army after a bitter struggle finally agreed to leave Washington.

MacArthur ordered that they be supplied with gasoline so they could drive out of the city.

The next morning MacArthur woke up to find himself the most unpopular man in the country next to President Hoover, who had issued the original order. Newspapers throughout the country featured the pictures of the immaculate General and his aide, and the dirty and malnourished Bonus Marchers being driven from their burning shacks. There were stories of the Army's supposedly cruel treatment of the veterans. Little attention was paid to MacArthur's report to Secretary Hurley that his men "neither suffered nor inflicted a serious casualty. They had not fired a shot and had actually employed no more dangerous weapons than harmless tear-gas bombs." Asked by reporters why he had worn a uniform so heavily bedecked with medals, MacArthur did not reply that this uniform had been sent to him from home. Instead, he replied, "Should I be ashamed of the medals? I earned each one in action."

When Franklin Delano Roosevelt was elected President in November, 1932, he and Douglas MacArthur were already old friends. This friendship had begun back in 1913 when Roosevelt was the young Assistant Secretary of the Navy and MacArthur was a major with the Army General Staff.

Even before Roosevelt moved into the White House, MacArthur let it be known that "the United States is now the seventeenth ranking nation in military strength." At first President Roosevelt ordered cuts in the Army's budget in order to lower government spending. With a personal friend in the White House, MacArthur had expected a change in attitude from the old pennypinching days. When he found out what the President had ordered he dropped in to see him one day. Soon the air was thick with argument. Roosevelt said sharply that it was his job as President to run the affairs of the country and he would cut the military budget. MacArthur in turn told him, "If you pursue this policy, I shall ask for my immediate relief as Chief of Staff and for retirement from the Army. And I shall take this fight directly to the people."

Roosevelt did not consider this as a threat, coming as it did from a friend. Instead, he gave serious consideration to the General's arguments. When he established the Civilian Conservation Corps (C.C.C.) to put unemployed to work on reforestation projects, he let MacArthur's officers run the 1,450 camps. He also permitted some relief money to be used to speed motorization of the field artillery.

MacArthur's four-year term as Chief of Staff was to expire in November, 1934. However, Roosevelt paid no attention to the four-year custom and insisted he stay on. "I must always find a way to keep Douglas close to me," he is reported to have said. "If we ever have another A.E.F., he's the man to take over."

The relationship between President Roosevelt and General MacArthur was closer than merely that of old social friends. Quite frequently the President called MacArthur to the White House to discuss legislation that did not deal with the military branch. Roosevelt admired the sharpness of his mind, his devotion to principles, and the ease with which he expressed himself.

"You seem willing to take my advice occasionally about almost everything except military matters," MacArthur told him one day. "Why is this, Mr. President?"

"Douglas," Roosevelt replied, "to me you are a symbol of the conscience of America."

MacArthur stayed on as Chief of Staff for an extra year.

Then one day during the summer of 1935, Manuel Quezon, who was in Washington, made an appointment to see President Roosevelt. The Tydings-McDuffie Act had been passed by Congress in 1934. It promised full independence to the Philippines by 1946. Quezon was soon to be inaugurated as the first President of the Philippine Commonwealth, which was to function until the day of independence.

Quezon insisted that General MacArthur help him establish the Philippines' defenses. It was with great reluctance that President Roosevelt agreed to let MacArthur go if the General wanted to.

However, even when MacArthur expressed his interest in serving as Quezon's military adviser, Roosevelt tried to change his mind. First he offered him the opportunity to remain on as Chief of Staff. MacArthur told him that this would deprive another officer of his rightful promotion. Then on September 3, 1935, President Roosevelt called MacArthur to have lunch with him at his home in Hyde Park, New York. Here he asked him to become the first United States High Commissioner to the Philippines. MacArthur turned this down, too, on the ground that his career had been in military and not civilian affairs.

Nevertheless, MacArthur did not accept Quezon's offer until Quezon agreed to one qualification. Only if Mrs. MacArthur could accompany him to Manila would he go. His mother was eighty-three years old and suffering from chronic heart trouble. However, her doctor said that her condition would not be affected by the 10,000-mile voyage to the Philippines.

Time was growing short now. On September 5th, MacArthur was called into the office of Secretary of War George

Dern. Here he was presented with a new medal. The citation read:

Douglas MacArthur, General, Chief of Staff, for exceptional meritorious and distinguished services in a position of great responsibility. As Chief of Staff since November 21, 1930, he has performed his important and exacting duties with signal success. He devised and developed a Four Army organization of our land forces, he conceived and established the General Headquarters air force, he initiated a comprehensive program of modernization in the Army's tactics, equipment, training organization. . . .

The most important part of General MacArthur's life was about to unfold.

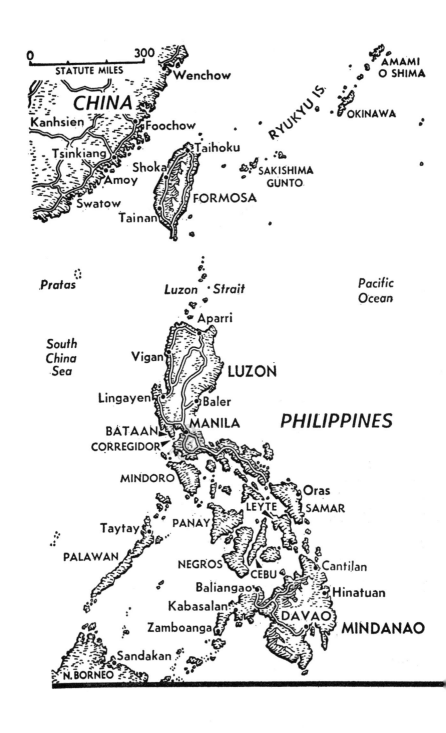

Chapter 8

ROAD TO BATAAN

SHORTLY before he departed for Manila, Douglas MacArthur met once more with President Roosevelt for a final talk. As he rose to leave the President's oval White House office, Roosevelt suddenly said with deep feeling, "Doug, if war comes, don't wait for orders to return here. Grab the first transportation you can find. I want you to command my armies."

It was the fall of 1935 when MacArthur walked up the gangway of the *President Hoover* in San Francisco. Besides his ailing mother, he was taking with him a small staff of men. For his Chief of Staff he had appointed Major Dwight D. Eisenhower. Major James Ord was to be Eisenhower's deputy. Eisenhower had served as MacArthur's aide since 1932, and his chief function was to write reports for the General. A 1915 graduate of West Point, Eisenhower had seen no service in World War I, but several ranking generals, including MacArthur, attested to his high ability. MacArthur also took with him Major Howard Hutter of the Army Medical Corps; Captain T. J. Davis, who was to be his per-

sonal aide; and two enlisted men as clerks. These few were
to form the nucleus of the Philippines' defense mission.

During the voyage across the Pacific, MacArthur worked
hard with Eisenhower and Ord in drafting a national defense act for the Philippines. This was his fourth assignment in the islands and no one knew better than MacArthur
the military problems involved. When Quezon had first
approached him about becoming his military adviser, he had
asked bluntly, "Can the Philippine Islands be defended?"

MacArthur had been frank in his reply. "I don't think
so," he told Quezon. "But they can be protected by the time
you get full independence in 1946—provided you have the
necessary money."

"What will be required?" Quezon asked anxiously.

"About eight million dollars in gold a year for the next
ten years." Even so, MacArthur also pointed out, the defense
of the islands would depend ultimately on naval and air
support by the United States.

By the time MacArthur reached Manila, he and his aides
had already drawn up a defense program for the Philippines.
Quezon quickly pushed it through his legislature and it
became Public Law No. I of the Commonwealth.

Shortly after MacArthur established his headquarters in
Manila, he was dealt a harsh blow. The long ocean trip had
done his mother no good. Once on land, her condition took a
decided turn for the worse. Adequate medicines were not
available. Dr. Hutter required a special serum, but it could
not be found in the Philippines. Frantically, MacArthur
radioed the United States for some. A Clipper plane was on
its way from California when she died early in December, 1935.

It was a deep blow to General MacArthur, who sorrowed

greatly upon his mother's death. For several weeks he was a recluse. But eventually the immense task facing him helped take his mind off his personal loss.

In addition, he now had a fiancée. On the ship traveling to the Orient, the captain had introduced him to Jean Marie Faircloth of Murfreesboro, Tennessee. MacArthur was immediately taken by her warm smile and her witty comments. He learned that her grandfather had fought on the Confederate side against his father at Missionary Ridge. At the stopover at Honolulu he had filled her stateroom with roses. At thirty-five, she was twenty years younger than he, but he felt relaxed and happy in her company.

Miss Faircloth was on her way to Manila, and MacArthur began to court her after his mother's death. They were married in April, 1937.

When he began his task as military adviser to Quezon, General MacArthur was well aware that the Philippine army was in reality only a meager police force. It consisted entirely of a few thousand Philippine scouts and a handful of trained officers, hardly a sufficient number to deter the aggressive Japanese military machine from trying to conquer the Philippines.

He mentioned his problem in a humorous but sharp way when he attended a dinner in his honor. Arriving at the club, he was greeted by two tattered young Filipinos who carried popguns. "I didn't know I had two soldiers to start out with," he said with a smile to his hosts.

MacArthur's national defense program for the Philippines proposed a trained citizens' militia of 400,000 men by 1946. Each year 40,000 recruits would be drafted and given five and a half months of training in the 128 camps he constructed. After a man completed his training he would become a member of a reserve division. At the end of ten years there would be forty divisions.

In addition to this army, MacArthur planned a fleet of fifty speedy patrol-torpedo boats (PT boats) to watch over the coastal area, as well as an air force of 250 planes, consisting of bomber, fighter and training planes. MacArthur also placed emphasis on building up the officer corps. In fact, shortly after his arrival in Manila, he lost no time in creating a military academy, using as his guide his old alma mater, West Point. He also laid out a plan for constructing vital fortifications and defense works.

President Quezon was so pleased with MacArthur's program that in August of 1936, he named him a field marshal. In private, Quezon pointed out that this honor was certainly due MacArthur. But in addition he believed that this gesture would help his nation's morale. For Filipinos loved dash and color, and the title of field marshal was much more impressive than that of general.

In a handsome ceremony in the very palace where he had once surrendered his sword to MacArthur's father, Quezon awarded MacArthur a field marshal's gold baton. To MacArthur, who had not asked for this title, it was a great honor, but a storm broke over this event both in the Philippines and back in the United States. In the Philippines, the pacifists and those isolationists who claimed that war would never come to their homeland protested MacArthur's $30,000 salary and his comfortable six-room air-conditioned penthouse atop the new Manila Hotel. Back in the War Department in Washington, the MacArthur detractors referred to him as the "Napoleon of the Islands." Because of the white sharkskin uniform he had worn at the ceremony, some called him the "dandy of the Philippines." They were

joined by a few newspaper editors, one of whom said the
following: "This bellicose, swashbuckling ex-chief of staff is
setting up a military dictatorship for his pal Quezon."

Accustomed to such backbiting, MacArthur took these
slanders in silence. As he well knew, the task he had set
up for himself required all his energy and he had none
to spare in defending himself against personal attacks. He
was soon to find out that the guns and equipment loaned
to him by the American Army were World War I relics,
many of them rusty or warped. He was shocked to learn
that the United States Navy considered PT boats a joke.
Only when he got in touch personally with Admiral William
D. Leahy, the Chief of Naval Operations, was he assured
that a few would be sent him. Nor could he count on acquiring planes as fast as he wanted them. As for the Filipino
recruits who were drafted, most were illiterate, in poor
health, or opposed to becoming part of a citizens' army
even for five and a half months. Much of that time had
to be spent teaching them hygiene, morals, and how to
exercise.

Because of these many problems, MacArthur was pleased
when word reached him from one of President Roosevelt's
assistants that the President wanted Quezon to visit him
at the White House in February, 1937. Quezon and Mac-
Arthur made the 10,000-mile trip, but on arriving Mac-
Arthur learned that President Roosevelt was not even aware
Quezon was in the United States, nor had he originally
made the request that Quezon come. When the President's
secretary refused to let MacArthur see the President, Mac-
Arthur went to the White House in a fury.

A short time later the red-faced secretary ushered him into
the President's office. "If you do not see Quezon," he told

Roosevelt during their two-hour talk, "all of Asia will take it as a sign that the United States has no interest in the Philippines. Furthermore, it is necessary to keep his friendship because many prominent Filipinos are pressuring him to give up the idea of independence." Roosevelt quickly agreed to meet with Quezon, who did not know what had occurred.

While in Washington, MacArthur was the guest at an affair. Many of his old Army colleagues were present when a speaker pointed toward MacArthur and told the story of a Marine captain who became a brigadier general of a small foreign army. When the Marine returned to Washington, he was invited to a party. He asked which uniform he should wear. He was told, "In Washington, a brigadier general of an army like yours eats in the kitchen." MacArthur remained quiet at the conclusion of the story, while the others present laughed uproariously.

Toward the end of 1937, General Malin Craig, who had succeeded MacArthur as Army Chief of Staff, wrote him that he was being recalled home. Quezon was shocked at this, for his program was still in its early stage. He insisted that MacArthur retire from the American Army and remain in the Philippines. MacArthur agreed, and on December 31 he retired from the service he so loved.

On February 21, 1938, MacArthur became the father of a son whom he named Arthur in honor of his father. The boy became the delight of his life. Before long he nicknamed him "The Sergeant," and friends who came visiting found the proud father giving the child piggyback rides and teaching him how to salute.

There was a sense of mission in his activities as that year progressed. The Japanese warlords were now deep in Manchuria and China and they spoke of a relentless drive to conquer all of Asia. MacArthur stood as the symbol of opposition to their plans. Japanese newspapers mentioned General MacArthur as the enemy and referred to him as if he were a mighty military force all by himself. Paul V. McNutt, U. S. High Commissioner to the Philippines, said, "I wouldn't hesitate to call President Quezon 'Manuel,' but I never called the General 'Doug.'"

In September of 1939, Hitler's Nazi armies crossed into Poland. MacArthur knew that World War II would soon envelop the globe, just as he had predicted shortly after World War I. Belatedly, Congress changed its view that he was a warmonger and took its first steps to increase the nation's defenses. But little equipment came his way because almost total emphasis was placed on helping England and France withstand the German war machine in Europe.

There were other troubles he faced. The Philippine legislature sharply cut its promised $8,000,000 annual defense budget. Instead of providing 40,000 men with meager military training each year, only 20,000 were drafted. More than that, entire tribes refused to register for the draft. "No small nation or great one," said MacArthur bluntly, "which is not willing to fight to the death for its freedom, is fit to enjoy it long."

By the summer of 1941, an air of imminent danger hung over the Philippines. Then the Japanese moved into Indochina and took over Hainan Island close to the Philippines. MacArthur was working later and later into the night, and paced the floor as he thought. Just before dawn one morning the hotel tenant directly under his suite called the manager to complain, "Doesn't that guy know what time it is?"

On July 26, President Roosevelt recalled MacArthur to

active duty and made him Commander of U. S. Army Forces in the Far East (USAFFE). In early October about thirty-five B-17 bombers arrived, as well as some ammunition. A few P-40 fighters also flew in. These were hardly enough to stem a tiny aggression, but the government's new rule of thumb was a single plane for MacArthur for every fifty sent to Europe.

On November 28, MacArthur received the following "alert" from Washington: "Negotiations with Japan appear to be terminated to all practical purposes, with only the barest possibility that the Japanese Government might come back and offer to continue. . . . If hostilities cannot be avoided the United States desires that Japan commit the first overt act."

General George C. Marshall was now Army Chief of Staff. He informed MacArthur that he did not believe the Japanese would attack before April, 1942, and advised him to make his plans accordingly. There would thus be ample time to strengthen the small defenses of the Philippines.

However, by the end of November, MacArthur's single radar set picked up Japanese planes flying over Luzon. The flights increased during the first week of December. Then at 4 A.M. on December 8, Asiatic time, MacArthur's phone rang. Havoc had rained down from early-morning skies at Pearl Harbor in Hawaii. War with Japan had arrived. MacArthur picked up his Bible and read it for a while. Then he rose for battle.

Chapter 9

"I SHALL RETURN"

Ten hours after the attack on Pearl Harbor, Japanese planes hit the Philippines. For months MacArthur had begged Washington for adequate radar cover. But with official concentration on the war in Europe only seven sets were sent him by the close of November. There had been time to put only a single set in operation before the Japanese attack.

In addition, MacArthur was able to accumulate only a handful of anti-aircraft guns. Their range was so short as to make them almost useless. His artillery ammunition was more than a decade old and had corroded fuses. As events disclosed, five out of every six of his three-inch shells were duds.

Nor was his meager air force able to engage the enemy. Except at the Del Monte field at Mindanao, hundreds of miles from Manila, he had lacked proper equipment to provide the wide, long runways necessary for bombers. Nevertheless, his B-17's took the risk of landing at Clark Field, some 65 miles from Manila, on Luzon. As for his seventy fighter planes, he had no spare parts for repair work.

Shortly before the Japanese attack, MacArthur had ordered General Lewis H. Brereton to send his thirty-five B-17's from Clark Field to the southern island of Mindanao. However, this order was not fully carried out. Instead, seventeen B-17's remained at Clark and these took off for patrol flights in the morning and the pilots landed at noon back at Clark Field for lunch. The field's radar set had not yet been installed, and without warning Japanese planes raced across the field in waves of fifty at a time. The rusty anti-aircraft guns proved useless. Before the Japanese flew away, seventeen bombers and forty fighters were destroyed on the ground. Some of the planes at Mindanao flew north to give fight to the Japanese planes. Most were shot down and those that were left flew to Australia, and were used in other battle areas.

When MacArthur reviewed the ruins, he realized that at a single blow he had lost half his tiny air strength. However, he refused to blame General Brereton, because sooner or later his planes would have been destroyed by the overwhelmingly superior Japanese air force.

So from the outset, the Japanese controlled the air over the Philippines. The extent of their air supremacy was revealed only two days later when at their leisure Japanese planes destroyed the Cavite Navy Yard on Manila Bay. From her penthouse apartment atop the Manila Hotel nine miles away, Mrs. MacArthur and three-year-old Arthur watched the bombings.

MacArthur was now left with an inadequate land force to stem the Japanese invasion he knew would soon be coming on Luzon Island. It was obvious to him that the chief objective of the enemy was to capture Manila Bay, the great prize on Luzon Island. Under the defense program called the "Orange Plan," MacArthur was to resist the Japanese invasion and prevent the capture of Manila Bay until the American Navy came to his rescue.

Unfortunately, his total army consisted of only 19,000 American officers and men, 20,000 Philippine regulars including 12,000 Filipino scouts, and whatever Filipino reserves he could call to the colors. The Japanese invasion force consisted of a minimum of 200,000 well-trained soldiers. To make matters even more unbalanced, the American Navy, having suffered great destruction at Pearl Harbor, had no intention of pitting itself against the Japanese navy at this time.

Another general might have given up at this point without a struggle. But MacArthur was made of sterner stuff. He had a partially equipped and trained force in northern Luzon under General Jonathan "Skinny" Wainwright, one in the south under General Jones, and local Philippine fighters in the southeast. "My concept for the initial defense of the Philippine Islands," he said, "was to defeat the enemy on the beaches where he would be at his weakest in any attempted amphibious landings." However, when the 200,000 Japanese landed on the north and south coasts of Luzon on December 10 and 12, expected American submarines were not in the vicinities.

There was only one answer now if he were to continue to resist successfully until naval and air aid came to his rescue. This was to bring his Luzon forces together on Bataan Peninsula and thus maintain control over Manila Bay. He would establish his headquarters on the rocky island fortress of Corregidor, three miles off Bataan Peninsula and controlling the entrance to Manila Bay.

In order to spare the 600,000 citizens of Manila from air bombings, on Christmas Eve MacArthur declared Manila an open city and evacuated his forces. Unfortunately, the Japanese took his declaration as an invitation and subjected Manila to full-scale air bombings. MacArthur's wife refused the opportunity to leave her husband, and together with her son and his Chinese nurse, Ah Chuh, set off from Manila across the bay westward to Corregidor. In her haste, she took little with her from the apartment besides some clothing. Just before walking out, she remembered her husband's medals, won over his career of forty years, and brought them with her.

MacArthur's fighting forces were now reduced to the Bataan Peninsula. The Japanese army had come down from the north of Luzon to the neck of Bataan Peninsula, which stretched only twenty miles from Subic Bay to Pampanga Bay. Ahead of them lay MacArthur's small force deployed in the swamp mud, matted underbrush and humid hillsides. Beyond them lay victory.

MacArthur's orders were to fight for every inch of the way. If the men could hold out only a few months, he assured them, help would come. Above, the Japanese dropped bombs. "Just three planes," MacArthur said angrily to his air aide, General Harold George. "I'm begging Washington for just three planes. Without them I am blind."

As the rain poured down steadily on Bataan, the men fought valiantly to stem the Japanese tide. Daily, MacArthur sent messages to Washington and pleaded for more equipment and a naval assault. Words of encouragement came in return—but no aid. Slowly a shortage of food developed. MacArthur had stocked Bataan with 150 days of rations for his 50,000 men. But the Japanese cleverly panicked the civilian population of Luzon and thousands of these poor people had run helter-skelter into the Peninsula.

MacArthur could not let them starve. The result was that his men were soon on half rations, then on quarter rations. All available mules and horses were slaughtered and eaten.

Inch by inch, MacArthur's army was slowly forced to fall back toward the southern part of the Peninsula. From Washington, MacArthur heard that his desired supplies could not get through the Japanese naval blockade. "A paper blockade," he described it in return. "The bulk of the Japanese navy, operating on tight schedules, was headed south for the seizure of Borneo, Malaya and Indonesia. American carriers could have approached the Philippines and unloaded some planes on fields still in our possession in Mindanao."

Back in Washington, Brigadier General Eisenhower, who had returned to the United States in 1939 after four years with MacArthur, was handling Philippine affairs for the Army. "A great nation such as ours," said Eisenhower, "no matter how unprepared for war, could not afford coldbloodedly to turn its back upon our Filipino wards." But the government's policy, though not expressed to MacArthur, was that the Philippines were expendable. Chief emphasis must be placed on the fighting in Europe.

Malaria, other tropical ailments and malnutrition hit MacArthur's forces. On Corregidor, MacArthur maintained his staff headquarters inside the dank, ill-smelling Malinta Tunnel. Despite the continual air attacks on the little island, he and his family lived in the open in a small house. When that house was destroyed, he moved to another house. During air raids he walked about without a regulation steel helmet. "I have no right to gamble my life," he admitted to an aide. "But it is absolutely necessary because of the effect all down the line. The soldiers say, 'I guess if the Old Man can take it, I can, too.' "

President Quezon had also come to Corregidor. The foul air in the tunnel where he stayed had brought on a recurrence of tuberculosis. He became so ill that he could not move about without a wheel chair. As he grew steadily weaker, he was all the more determined to end the fighting. One day he proposed to MacArthur that he declare his country independent of the United States and ask Japan to treat the Philippines as a neutral nation.

So insistent did he become that MacArthur feared he would make this announcement on his own. To head him off, MacArthur agreed to forward his proposal to President Roosevelt. To this wire, MacArthur added a special message for the President. "Since I have no air or sea protection," he wrote, "you must be prepared at any time to figure on the complete destruction of this command. You must determine whether the mission of delay would be better furthered by the temporizing plan of Quezon or by my continued battle effort. The temper of the Filipinos is one of almost violent resentment against the United States. Every one of them expected help, and when it has not been forthcoming they believe they have been betrayed in favor of others."

President Roosevelt replied on February 9, 1942. He rejected Quezon's proposal, but gave MacArthur authority to surrender the Filipino soldiers under him. He also said, "American forces will continue to keep our flag flying in the Philippines so long as there remains any possibility of resistance."

Sick and weak as they were, and with dwindling ammunition, MacArthur's men continued to hold off the Japanese.

In other areas of the Far East, the Japanese took Hong Kong and Singapore and moved into other supposedly strong Allied territories. The stand of MacArthur's army was the only bright spot in the entire Allied cause. Back in the United States, his praises were heralded from one end of the country to the other. Said Secretary of War Stimson: "They exacted losses from the enemy that left no doubt in any mind of the quality of the American soldier."

During those dark days on Bataan, Prime Minister Winston Churchill visited President Roosevelt at the White House. Talk turned to the fighting prowess of General MacArthur. Churchill showed Roosevelt a copy of his orders to Viscount Gort, commanding general of the British expeditionary force at the enormous Dunkirk defeat. His orders to Gort were to return to England and turn over his command. "It would be a needless triumph for the enemy unless you do to MacArthur precisely what I did to Gort."

On February 22, Roosevelt sent a message to MacArthur, ordering him to leave Corregidor and go to Australia, which was to become the central base for fighting the Japanese. Roosevelt named MacArthur commander of the South-West Pacific Area.

"This order I must disobey," MacArthur told his staff. He argued that if he deserted his men, the name of the United States would be harmed throughout Asia. It was like asking the captain to be the first off his burning vessel.

President Quezon was too ill to remain inside the foul-smelling tunnel. Nor could he chance living in the open under continual air bombing. MacArthur made arrangements to send him to Australia, but he would not accompany him. This was an opportunity for Mrs. MacArthur to leave with her son. However, she rejected her husband's request with, "We three are one. We drink from the same cup."

Beleaguered as he was, MacArthur still believed that aid would be forthcoming and his brave soldiers would be saved. Wire after wire continued to pepper Washington for help, but none came. As the days drifted by, President Roosevelt grew exasperated with MacArthur because he would not leave his men. Finally, on March 10, he sent an angry message: "Leave immediately!"

MacArthur had no alternative now other than to obey the President's command. He took a walk with General Wainwright and told him he would be his successor. "We're all alone, Jonathan," he said glumly. "You know that as well as I." His voice grew stern with purpose. "If I get through to Australia, you know I'll come back as soon as I can with as much as I can. In the meantime, you've got to hold." He turned away with tears in his eyes.

On March 11th, four 65-foot motor torpedo boats arrived at Corregidor just as night fell. MacArthur had a terrible decision to make. He could take only nineteen members of his staff aboard the rusty boats. Whether these men departed with him or remained did not seem to make much difference because there was at best only one chance in five that these open boats could elude the Japanese. MacArthur might have traveled out by submarine as had President Quezon, but he had rejected underwater travel.

Mrs. MacArthur brought along only two small suitcases; one contained clothing and the other, food. One of the suitcases bore a tag which read, NEW GRAND HOTEL—YOKOHAMA. MacArthur decided to take little Arthur's nurse, Ah Chuh, with him because she would be tortured if captured by the Japanese. Ah Chuh, ever watchful of her four-year-old charge, carried her belongings in a large handker-chief. Before the four PT's departed, MacArthur took a last look at the "grim, gaunt, ghastly men" he was leaving behind. Then to lighten the situation, he called out, "We will go with the fall of the moon; we will go during the Ides of March." And to "Skinny" Wainwright he said solemnly, "I shall return."

The four boats were to travel to their early-morning ren-dezvous at uninhabited Cuyo Islands. From here they were to make a watery trip to the far-off Mindanao meeting place. Then planes were to carry them to Australia.

Nothing came off as planned. Japanese mine fields and rough seas separated the boats. One PT went on alone to Cagayan, on the north coast of Mindanao. MacArthur's boat ran out of fuel and his party transferred to another PT at the Cuyos. Then on the way to Mindanao, a Japanese warship suddenly hove into sight at the horizon. The en-gines were cut and the men waited for their doom. But the Japanese did not spy them and soon passed out of sight.

At Mindanao, MacArthur's party was to be met by four Flying Boxcars. "We learned," said MacArthur, "that of the four planes dispatched, only one had arrived and that without brakes or superchargers, and being unfit for its mis-sion, it had already departed." The result was a three-day wait under tense conditions, with the Japanese aware that MacArthur was on Mindanao.

Finally on March 16, two planes flew in and landed at the makeshift camouflaged airfield. At midnight began a seven-hour flight across Japanese-conquered East Indies, New Guinea and Timor.

The planes landed at Batchelor Field at Darwin, Australia, during an air raid. MacArthur's face was drawn, but his expression was determined when he stepped out of the plane. "I came through," he said with emotion, "and I shall return!"

Chapter 10

BEGINNING OF THE COMEBACK

IT was General MacArthur's understanding that he had been ordered to leave his men on Bataan and Corregidor so that he could lead the war in the Pacific against the Japanese Empire. He assumed that a large and well-trained military force awaited his arrival in Australia to begin the gigantic task.

Shortly after his plane touched down at Darwin, he turned to an American officer stationed in Australia. His first thought was to save the men he had left behind in the Philippines. "How large are the United States forces assembled in Australia for the Philippines rescue mission?" he asked.

The officer turned his head away. "As far as I know, sir, there are very few troops here," was his reply.

"Surely this officer must be in error," MacArthur said to General Richard Sutherland, his chief of staff, who had traveled from Corregidor with him.

Exhausted as he was, MacArthur flew south from that hot, sandy airfield to Alice Springs, three hours away. Then he boarded a rickety train to Melbourne across the long burning desert of Australia. He had dispatched General Richard

Marshall, his deputy chief of staff, on a mission to learn the truth about his military strength in Australia. At Adelaide, Marshall climbed aboard the train. "Well, what do we have?" MacArthur greeted him.

"There are only 25,000 American soldiers in all of Australia," Marshall told him. "This is less than half what we had on Bataan."

"I know," said MacArthur keenly disappointed.

"But even worse," Marshall continued, "they are poorly trained and you don't have infantry or tanks—only two National Guard coast artillery anti-aircraft regiments, some field artillery men, and two regiments of engineers."

"What about the Air Force?" asked MacArthur.

"About 250 planes, and most are not in flying condition."

"How about the Australian army?"

"Three divisions of their best men are on the North African desert. Also, the Australians here are panicky. They are certain that the Japanese will stage an invasion soon and they are planning on leaving all the northern ports open to the Japanese without a fight."

MacArthur's face turned the color of chalk. He was the general of an almost nonexistent military force. "It was the greatest shock and surprise of the whole war," he later admitted.

"I have never seen him so affected. He was heartbroken," said an aide.

"God have mercy on us," MacArthur said finally.

All that night he paced the narrow corridor of the train. He thought of his promise to General Wainwright to return soon to the Philippines in strength and drive the Japanese out of the islands.

In the early morning the train pulled into Melbourne.

An enormous crowd had collected hours before to greet him, and they cheered him as if he were a conquering hero. He was also surprised to learn from the officials who met him that back in the United States he was a great national hero. However, he knew that courage in defeat was never equal to victory and he spoke frankly to the throng:

"I have every confidence in the ultimate success of our joint cause. But success in modern warfare requires something more than courage and willingness to die. No general can make something out of nothing. My success or failure will depend primarily upon the resources which the respective governments place at my disposal. In any event, I shall do my best. I shall keep the soldier's faith."

The American Congress and President Roosevelt presented MacArthur with the Congressional Medal of Honor for his brave defense in the Philippines. However, he did not intend to sit back in satisfaction with the highest honor his nation could bestow on a soldier. "Let's get on with the war," he said when he was notified.

MacArthur's first order of business was to aid the forces he had left behind on Bataan. Having taken Singapore, the Japanese were shipping battle-hardened troops from that theater to the Philippines. By April first, they had begun a full-scale drive to conquer all of Bataan. In desperation, MacArthur wired the War Department of a bold plan to save the Bataan defenders. With whatever military strength he could muster he would swing around Bataan and attack the Japanese rear. He would take personal charge, he said, "if in your opinion my presence would help."

The War Department rejected both the plan and MacArthur's offer to return. A week later when Bataan fell, he wept openly. "The Bataan force went out as it wished —fighting to the end of its flickering, forlorn hope. No army has ever done so much with so little. Nothing became it like its last hour of trial and agony," he said.

Early in May the last resistance on the island of Corregidor ended. The Philippines now belonged to Japan. "Corregidor needs no comment from me," he said. "It has sounded its own story at the mouth of its guns."

His great objective became that of liberating the Philippines. However, he realized the enormity of this task. His most immediate job was to change the deep defeatism he found among the seven million citizens of Australia. Without a build-up base in this country, his assignment would be almost impossible to fulfill. He met with Australia's political leaders and spoke optimistically of the future. He also addressed the Australian people to dispel the fog of defeat in the atmosphere.

The Australian military leaders spoke about "holding the 'Brisbane Line.'" This was a line running from Brisbane on the east-central coast to Adelaide on the southern coast, a small triangle of populated land. They were willing to give up three-fourths of Australia to the Japanese before taking defensive action. "We shall make the fight for Australia in New Guinea!" MacArthur said sternly, referring to the large island north of Australia. Holding the Brisbane Line, he said, was a concept "fatal to every possibility of ever assuming the offensive." To MacArthur, wars were won by conceiving and carrying out offensives and not defenses.

It was MacArthur's hope to command the unified land-sea-air forces for the entire Pacific fighting against Japan. However, in Washington the Navy impressed President Roosevelt with the argument that the Pacific fighting would be done chiefly on the ocean with amphibious raids along the way. From his great distance away from Washington, MacArthur insisted that the admirals were wrong. This angered the admirals. Some referred to him as "Dugout Doug" and claimed that he had hid in the tunnels on Corregidor during the fighting. Others said that he had deserted his men on Bataan. Said Secretary of War Stimson, "The Navy's astonishing bitterness against him seemed childish." Nevertheless, the Navy came away with a large share of the Pacific command. The vast Central Pacific Area became the hunting ground of Admiral Chester W. Nimitz, while first Admiral Robert L. Ghormley and then Admiral William F. "Bull" Halsey controlled the fighting in the South Pacific. MacArthur's zone was limited to the South-West Pacific Area, going from Australia through the Philippines in the north and from the Solomon Islands to Sumatra in the west.

MacArthur was willing to serve under another military officer if the different commands were combined under a single leader. However, President Roosevelt would not agree to this. Said MacArthur: "It was accepted and entirely successful in the other great theaters. The failure to do so in the Pacific . . . resulted in divided effort, waste, duplication and undue extension of the war."

There was still another factor affecting strategy in the Pacific. The European theater had priority over the Pacific. This mean that British and Russian allies had first call on American arms and equipment. MacArthur burned the wires to Washington for a fairer share. "Must I always lead a forlorn hope?" he asked.

Finally, on April 6, 1942, the untrained 41st National Guard Infantry Division landed in Australia. The following month came the 32nd Division, as well as experienced Australian brigades from the African desert. With this small force MacArthur believed he could go on the offensive.

"The Poor Man's War," was the way his aides referred to his proposed line of action, while others called it "Operation Shoestring." While the Australian government expected momentary invasion, MacArthur's plan was to "stop the enemy advances along the Owen Stanley Range in New Guinea." He knew that if he were successful the Japanese would be unable to invade Australia. Morale, sunk so low since Pearl Harbor, would immediately shoot upward.

The Japanese were in control of Rabaul with its excellent air and naval bases on the northern tip of New Britain, the large island north and east of New Guinea. Rabaul was to serve as their major base for their step-by-step advance toward and into Australia. From Rabaul they had captured Lae and Salamaua on the eastern coast of New Guinea. MacArthur knew that their next objective was Port Moresby, which lay southward across the Owen Stanley Range, about 350 miles from Australia.

It was on May 3rd that the Japanese sent aircraft carriers around New Guinea's southern tip to take Port Moresby by amphibious action. However, an American task force met them near Milne Bay and the Battle of the Coral Sea took place. The result was an American victory that brought temporary abandonment of the Japanese attempt to take Port Moresby. This was the strangest naval battle in the world's history, for not a single ship fired a shot. Instead, all the action was provided by carrier-based planes that sank three Japanese and one American aircraft carriers.

Only a month later when the Japanese attempted to take the island of Midway, Admiral Nimitz's carrier task force met them and his planes sank four more Japanese aircraft carriers. The importance of the Battle of Midway was that for the first time since Pearl Harbor the American Navy was again more powerful than the Japanese navy. By no means however, did this imply that the Japanese navy was now weak.

At the time of the Midway engagement, MacArthur was living in an apartment in the Lennon Hotel in Brisbane. Many of his top staff officers also lived at the Lennon, and when the day's planning work had been completed at their headquarters building, they met frequently at night in MacArthur's fourth-floor apartment to continue their work. Mrs. MacArthur cooked all of his meals. Breakfast came at seven-thirty sharp, but she had no way of knowing when he would appear for his evening meal.

Toward the end of July, MacArthur was working far into the night and dinner was now more uncertain than ever. From Washington had come orders for a triple offensive. The first part of the attack was to start at Guadalcanal at the south end of the Solomon Islands on August 7. This attack would be led by Admiral Halsey and occupation would be attempted by the Marines. Guadalcanal was considered to be lightly held by the Japanese, though action was to last six months until February, 1943. Part two would be the capture of Lae and Salamaua on New Guinea's east coast. Then would come action at Rabaul.

MacArthur's timetable was upset on July 22 when word came that the Japanese had captured Gona and Buna, forward bases on the east coast of New Guinea only 100 miles from Port Moresby. Most surprising of all, a large Japanese force was attempting to cross over the 14,000-foot-high Owen Stanley Range and storm into Port Moresby. Should Port

Moresby now fall, all of Australia would be within reach of the enemy.

MacArthur established his forward headquarters at Port Moresby at this time to direct the war against the oncoming Japanese. It was hard to imagine that this junction should be a most valuable military goal. The native policemen wore red-blanket sarongs, and what MacArthur saw was "a native village, huts on stilts in the shallow coastal waters" and "tropical cottages with wide verandas and corrugated-iron roofs." For his residence MacArthur selected a bungalow that had an enormous library of fiction and nonfiction books in several languages. Often when his staff officers came to see him, he would either be pacing the floor, a corncob pipe in his mouth and a map in his hand, or he would be reading one of the books of his library.

On July 28th, Major General George C. Kenney arrived to take over the Fifth Air Force under MacArthur. There had been talk that MacArthur was disgusted with his air support because of its lack of achievement in the Pacific fighting. He looked angry as he spoke with Kenney, but the airman refused to bow or scrape or make humble apology. MacArthur's approach was just a show to test whether Kenney would stand up for himself. Finally MacArthur walked over and threw an arm around Kenney's shoulder. "George, I think we are going to get along together all right," he said with a smile. An old colonel who had served several years under MacArthur summed up for Kenney the staff opinion of the man: "Douglas MacArthur is a hard-boiled old softie."

MacArthur told Kenney that on August 7th the South Pacific Marines were to land on Guadalcanal and Tulagi. He believed that these landings were unnecessary and would not be worth the price of the American blood lost in their capture. However, he told Kenney, he was expected to help the First Marine Division with his available air and naval support. Furthermore, the Japanese on New Guinea were making headway across the Owen Stanley heights and Kenney would be expected to deal with them.

Not long after he arrived, Kenney reported to MacArthur again. He had found sixty-two B-17 bombers under his command but only six planes were in combat condition. MacArthur looked glum because the Japanese air force was daily bombing his advanced headquarters' zone. From Rabaul, the Japanese were flying south in complete control of the air over New Guinea and the Solomons where the Marines were to land. "I'll have between sixteen and eighteen B-17's over Rabaul by August seventh," Kenney assured MacArthur.

Early on the morning of August 7th, as the Marines were preparing to land at Guadalcanal, Kenney had fifteen B-17's racing toward Rabaul. Up to that time, this was the biggest air attack mustered by the Americans in the Pacific. When his fliers returned, Kenney wore a broad grin. Of the 150 Japanese planes lined up off the Rabaul runway, Kenney's men destroyed seventy-five and damaged most of the others. In the air they shot down eleven of twenty Japanese fighters. The American loss was a single bomber. There would be no Japanese air attacks on the Marines landing that morning.

MacArthur's two American divisions were still undergoing training when the Japanese captured Gona and Buna on the east coast of New Guinea and started across the Owen Stanley Range for Port Moresby. He could muster only a small force of Australian soldiers, who found themselves outnumbered ten to one. The Australians gave ground steadily over the cloud-heavy limestone mountain passes and through the equatorial rain valleys and forests. "We shall win or we shall die," MacArthur said.

While the Japanese were advancing toward Port Moresby over the mountains, MacArthur reasoned that if he were the enemy he would attempt to outflank that base from another direction. The logical point would be at Milne Bay at the southeastern tip of New Guinea. He had hardly sent some troops there when the Japanese arrived. The fierce battle lasted a week and the Japanese were badly defeated. As for the Japanese force coming over the mountains, it arrived at a point only twenty-two miles from Port Moresby. However, jungle diseases and air attacks took their toll and they could not continue. A ragged lot by now, their remnants staggered back the way they had come.

It was MacArthur's turn now to take the offensive. Buna and Gona, the supply centers for the Japanese thrust at Port Moresby, had to be captured to relieve the pressure on that vital southern base. General Kenney solved the problem of how to bring the 32nd Division to New Guinea by flying the men 1,000 miles from their training center at Rockhampton, Australia. Then close to Buna, his fliers delivered an Army field hospital to care for expected casualties.

This was wretched country for warfare. There were swamps with crocodiles and deadly snakes, malaria and other tropical diseases awaited the men, and the heat was like a furnace. One of the generals noticed that MacArthur never looked wilted. "The sun poured down mercilessly," he said, "and my uniform was soggy and dark with wetness. I remember to my astonishment that General MacArthur, despite the heat and the vigorous exercise, did not perspire at all."

By late November of 1942, the Americans were stalled only

miles from Buna. Sick from malaria, the heat and lack of adequate food, the men suffered a serious drop in morale. There was only one way to take Buna and that was by a frontal attack, for MacArthur lacked a fleet to bombard Buna from the sea or transports to bring in his army from a side direction.

MacArthur disliked a frontal attack because his chief approach to fighting was to save his own forces from unnecessary casualties. But here at Buna there was no alternative except through frontal attack. Quickly he dispatched Lieutenant General Robert L. Eichelberger to take over the command and restore troop spirit and morale. He told him to replace every poor officer in the command and to give sergeants command of battalions if they were good leaders. "Bob, get me Buna—or don't come back alive!" he said in farewell.

Within a week Eichelberger roused his exhausted and discouraged men. Then on December 14, his force overran Buna, while the Australians took Gona.

As 1942 came to a close, MacArthur could look back on the most hectic year of his life. From Bataan to Buna, he had traveled from miserable defeat to the first major victory in the Pacific. Still far ahead of him lay the Philippines, but there was the first glimmer of hope that he would eventually be able to make his promised return.

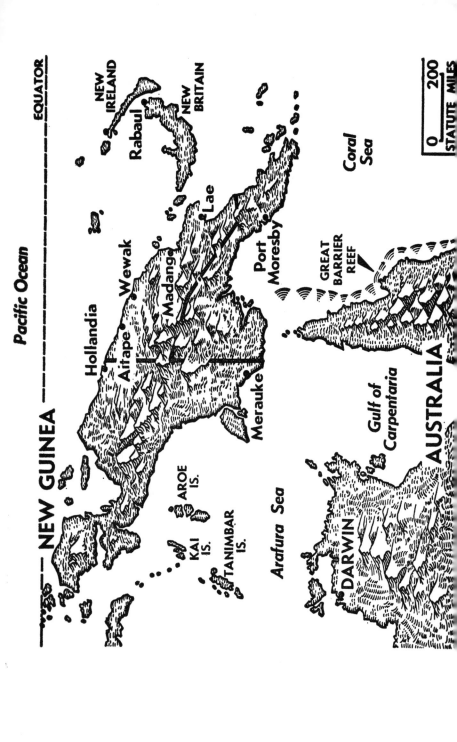

Chapter 11

IN SIGHT OF THE PHILIPPINES

For the year 1943, MacArthur set for himself the major goal of isolating the Japanese-held bastion of Rabaul near the northeastern tip of New Britain. In the previous year's fighting, General Kenney's surprise air attack had destroyed a great many planes there. But more had flown in, and many ships laden with men and equipment crowded that area. So long as Rabaul remained the nerve center of Japanese activities in the South Pacific MacArthur could not lay concrete plans for his return to the Philippines.

He was well aware of the major difficulties that faced him as 1943 began. Although military production had begun to zoom in the United States, he could not count on getting more than a small share for his theater of action. Outnumbered as his forces were by the enemy, he also realized that the Japanese were superb soldiers who fought bravely and recklessly to the end. For example, though he considered the Buna-Gona campaign finished by the beginning of the year, the uncaptured enemy soldiers at Sanananda in that zone put up three further weeks of fanatical fighting until they were subdued.

There were others problems. The mosquitoes of the jungles were responsible for more casualties than bullets. Entire battalions were laid low by malaria. MacArthur turned this problem, as well as all health matters, over to Colonel Howard "Doc" Smith, who had been Manila's health officer. Doc set up a system to inspect kitchens and messes and he had General Kenney fly in fresh meat from Australia. So far as the anopheles mosquito problem was concerned, the important work was done in laboratories back in the United States. Yet it was not until late in 1944 that the malaria rate fell sharply. MacArthur compared the successful fight against the anopheles mosquito with the victory over yellow fever in the construction of the Panama Canal.

Still another problem MacArthur faced was his lack of reliable information regarding the enemy. He lacked road maps, familiarity with landmarks to guide Kenney's planes, and the ability to translate captured enemy documents. An immediate help to him was the organization of Coast Watchers. These were men who went behind Japanese lines with radio transmitters and reported on troop movements as well as on air and sea programs. MacArthur also employed hundreds of Nisei, or Americans of Japanese descent, to translate captured Japanese maps, diaries and reports.

After the costly struggle for Buna, MacArthur was determined to make no more frontal assaults on the Japanese. His great desire was for victory, but with it was his hope to preserve his men for postwar civilian life. In keeping with this philosophy he developed the strategy of bypassing strong Japanese centers. Some military men mistakenly called this "island-hopping." But island-hopping was hitting one enemy center and then moving on to the next enemy stronghold. Instead, MacArthur's system was "leapfrogging."

A Japanese colonel later explained leapfrogging in this way: "This was the type of strategy we hated most. The Americans attacked and seized, with minimum losses, a relatively weak area, constructed air fields and then proceeded to cut the supply lines to our troops in that area. Our strong points were gradually starved out. The Japanese army preferred direct assault after the German fashion, but the Americans flowed into our weaker points and submerged us, just as water seeks the weakest entry to sink a ship."

MacArthur's entire strategy regarding the powerful Japanese base at Rabaul was based on leapfrogging. At an early meeting he met with his staff who were concerned with the heavy casualties that would result in taking Rabaul. Said one general: "I don't see how we can take Rabaul with our limited forces."

MacArthur smiled. "Well, let's just say that we won't take it. In fact, gentlemen, I don't want it." He turned to Kenney. "You incapacitate Rabaul," he said.

However, this was to happen far in the future. The immediate problem was what to do about the large reinforcements the Japanese were sending to New Guinea and the Solomon Islands from Rabaul.

Dealing with them became General Kenney's task, for MacArthur lacked a fleet to give sea battle to the Japanese. "Watch for the next 'front' of heavy weather," MacArthur told him. "That's when the Japanese will send a large convoy from Rabaul across the Bismarck Sea to reinforce Lae and Salamaua up the east coast of New Guinea."

To prepare for this even, Kenney put his fliers through hard maneuvers. For days they practiced skip bombing, or swooping in low near a target and then releasing bombs which skipped across the water to the vessel's hull. Carefully,

Kenney picked the exact site where he would attack the Japanese convoy, "a location where all our units could engage the Nips with the maximum efficiency. Three days before the battle, we rehearsed at full scale. We selected a half-submerged wreck that was exactly the same distance from our bases as the forthcoming engagement. Our units took off from their various fields at the same time they would take off three days later and we duplicated our flying problems in every possible manner, even to the formation and compass headings into the attack."

On March first, reconnaissance planes spotted a large Japanese convoy from Rabaul off Cape Gloucester. This was a convoy delivering 7,000 men and four months' food for 20,000 men to New Guinea. The next day Kenney's air raiders broke through the heavy, dark clouds over the Bismarck Sea and pounced on the twenty-two ships of the convoy. The three-day assault by his land-based planes wiped out almost the entire convoy and only 800 Japanese soldiers survived. MacArthur said of Kenney, "George was born three hundred years too late. He's just a natural-born pirate."

The Battle of the Bismarck Sea had a deep effect upon Japanese strategy thereafter. The experience so shook them that never again would they transport large forces of troops within the range of MacArthur's air power. The Bismarck Sea Battle also reinforced MacArthur's view that leapfrogging would depend "upon securing air control over the area covered in each forward step."

On February 8, 1943, Admiral Halsey had finally won control of Guadalcanal from the Japanese. Now he was shifted to MacArthur's strategic command. MacArthur had never met "Bull" Halsey and he wondered whether the Navy's general dislike of him would be evident in Halsey. However, he need not have had any concern, for Halsey took to him immediately. Said Halsey: "My mental picture poses him against the background of . . . discussions; he is pacing his office, almost wearing a groove between his large, bare desk and the portrait of George Washington that faced it; his corncob pipe in his hand (I rarely saw him smoke it); and he is making his points in a diction I have never heard surpassed."

MacArthur unfolded his plan to Halsey. He would approach Rabaul from New Guinea while Halsey would come up via the Solomon Islands. "Always hit them where they ain't," he explained his strategy of bypassing strong Japanese points. Cut off or left in the rear, these strong centers would die on the vine because fresh supplies and men would not be able to reach them. Halsey quickly grasped MacArthur's strategy, though Washington military strategists questioned his plan for leaving thousands upon thousands of Japanese soldiers behind in his rear areas. Even when his plan was long in operation they continued to question it.

However, as MacArthur repeatedly explained, those Japanese forces represented no menace to him. "Their capacity for organized offensive effort has passed. The actual process of their immediate destruction by assault methods would unquestionably involve heavy loss of life, without adequately compensating strategic advantages."

To lay the groundwork for his leapfrogging operations, MacArthur spent part of his time at his Brisbane headquarters and the rest with his men at advanced headquarters in the field. No matter where he was, his hoped-for return to the Philippines was always on his mind. Every headquarters building he named "Bataan" and the telephone exchange was always named "Corregidor." When he got a private plane he quickly ordered the name "Bataan" printed on its nose. His headquarters aides knew him as an unusual executive. He would tolerate no telephone in his office, nor would he employ a private secretary. If he wanted to talk to an aide, he walked to his office for a quick conference.

MacArthur's first major effort at leapfrogging came in the Lae-Salamaua zone far above Buna and Gona on the east coast of New Guinea. Instead of marching up the coast, he decided to make the first use of paratroopers in the Pacific. These were to land by surprise not far from Lae and seize the airport area, while amphibious forces would walk ashore on fairly unprotected beaches on the opposite side of the village.

When the time came for the paratroop drop on September fifth, MacArthur insisted upon riding in the leading plane. His staff protested but MacArthur overruled them. "I want to provide such comfort as my presence might bring to our paratroopers on their first combat mission," he said stubbornly. But to General Kenney, he added, "I'm not worried about getting shot. The only thing that disturbs me is the possibility that when we hit the rough air over the mountains, my stomach might get upset. I'd hate to get sick and disgrace myself in front of the kids."

When the paratroop drops and the amphibious landings on the beach worked as planned, MacArthur wired his wife in Brisbane, "It was a honey." Recovering from the surprise, the Japanese moved to attack the amphibious forces. But MacArthur ordered more men brought in by air in their rear. Soon the Japanese did not know which way to turn and Lae fell to the Americans.

With the loss of Lae, the Japanese expected MacArthur to strike next farther up the New Guinea coast. In fact, he ordered word passed along to Japanese spies that he planned to do so. However, he advised Admiral Halsey to make the next move in the Solomons. Leapfrogging over the strongly held Japanese point at Kolombangara, Halsey went halfway up the Solomons and took Vella Lavella.

What followed was more of the same. Repeatedly, Mac-Arthur let the Japanese spend energy and manpower building up the next logical place they assumed he would attack. Then instead he would bypass those places and leave them to wither on the vine by cutting off their supply lines. The Japanese never knew where his forces would appear.

For instance, the Japanese worked feverishly to safeguard their strong center at Buin-Faisi on Bougainville, the top island of the Solomons. MacArthur did land troops on Bougainville, but he put them at Empress Augusta Bay above Buin-Faisi. Then he had Kenney's planes race to Rabaul where they destroyed 177 planes that could have seriously interfered with his surprise move. This double action doomed more than 50,000 Japanese soldiers who were left behind to the south in the Solomons.

Between New Guinea and New Britain lay the vital Vitiaz Strait. Until MacArthur controlled these waters he could not move ships through to take possession of northern New Guinea and acquire close bases for his eventual thrust at the Philippines.

For this task, he made use of Lieutenant General Walter Krueger, who had gone up the ranks from private to his high position. Krueger, a daring fighter, commanded the Sixth Army. First, Finschhafen, a busy enemy port that guarded the western side of Vitiaz Strait on New Guinea, was taken. Then Krueger put his men ashore at Arawe across the Strait on New Britain, at the opposite end of the large island from Rabaul. When the Japanese rushed troops to Arawe, the Americans struck at Cape Gloucester, eighty miles away. By now the Japanese were concerned that MacArthur would attempt to capture Rabaul and they diverted men from the field to that center. However, MacArthur had no intention of making a frontal assault on Rabaul. Instead, he first established control of Rabaul's right by taking Green Island. Then he took Emirau Island on its left flank. Rabaul was now surrounded and could no longer function as the chief Japanese base in the Southwest Pacific.

At the beginning of 1944, MacArthur was able to judge with satisfaction how well his strategy of leapfrogging had worked. He had taken almost 800,000 square miles of Japanese-held territory, isolated tens of thousands of the enemy's soldiers, and had gained control of the important Vitiaz Strait. All this had come with only a small loss in his own ranks.

However, the Philippines lay almost 1,500 miles away to the north and west and there still was a mountainous task ahead of him. As the new year dawned, he set for himself two immediate jobs. Above New Guinea and New Britain was the Bismarck Sea. Here at its head lay the Admiralty Islands, composed of forty tiny islands and the large island of Manus with an excellent harbor and airfields. The Japanese would hardly expect him to attack Manus because it was so far away. Yet MacArthur knew that Manus would be a superb advance base to provide cover for his second immediate objective. This was to clear the long northern coast of New Guinea and put him hundreds of miles closer to the Philippines.

Although his staff aides protested that taking Manus was too dangerous an undertaking, MacArthur insisted that it be done. On February 24, 1944, he set sail with Vice Admiral Thomas C. Kinkaid's amphibious forces and a few days later the troops hit the shore at Manus. Before he had left his advance base, General Kenney had said to MacArthur, "I sure hope that the Japanese cleared the mud off the runways before they laid their surface of coral. Otherwise, we won't be able to land heavy planes." MacArthur had promised to look into this matter.

Japanese snipers lay hidden in the tall grass alongside the airfield at Manus and shot at the landing troops. Disregarding this fire, MacArthur calmly walked up and down the airfield and was clearly distinguishable by his light trench coat and field marshal's cap. A jittery officer wanted him to return to the landing barge. "Excuse me, sir," he said, "but we killed a sniper in there only a few minutes ago."

"Fine," replied MacArthur. "That's the best thing to do with them."

Then he said to an aide as the bullets sang past them, "Let's dig into this coral surfacing and see how deep it is. I promised I'd give General Kenney a report." After careful digging, he found only two to three inches of coral. "I'm afraid General Kenney isn't going to like this," he said sadly.

At this point, the Japanese soldiers had crawled even closer. Afterward General Krueger grumbled, "They might well have got him." But MacArthur walked over to another general and said encouragingly, "You've got your teeth into the enemy now. Don't let him go."

By March 9, the 4,000 Japanese soldiers on Manus were subdued and the entire island was in American hands. After the action, MacArthur reported to Washington, "We have landed in the Admiralty Islands which stand at the northern entrance to the Bismarck Sea almost due south of Guam and

1,300 miles from the Philippines. The axis of advance has thereby been changed from the north to the west. This relieves our supply line of the constant threat of flank attack."

Without great danger, MacArthur was now able to leapfrog westward along the northern coast of New Guinea into Dutch New Guinea on the western part of the island that was three times the size of the Philippines.

About 250 miles westward from General Kenney's advance air base near the Vitiaz Strait lay Wewak. This was a large and crowded Japanese base and here the Japanese expected MacArthur's next attack on northern New Guinea. Instead, MacArthur planned to take Hollandia, 450 miles farther west.

In April he sent 300 ships from Manus and on the twenty-second, 66,000 men swarmed ashore at Hollandia. Taken by complete surprise, the Japanese at Hollandia fell easy victims to the invaders. A Japanese admiral had gone by submarine from Wewak to Hollandia to escape the supposed MacArthur attack on Wewak. Now when he saw the Americans on the beaches of Hollandia, he walked into the jungle and killed himself.

By taking Hollandia, MacArthur cut off 60,000 Japanese soldiers to his rear. No longer would the Japanese be able to send supplies from the Philippines to New Guinea.

After Hollandia came the capture of Wakde Islands, 110 miles closer to the Philippines. Then came Biak, which, said MacArthur, gave him "command domination of Dutch New Guinea except for isolated enemy positions." Next came Noemfoor, then Sansapor, then Morotai. Now MacArthur's men were only 300 miles from the southern island of Mindanao in the Philippines! He had come more than 2,000 miles on his return journey.

MacArthur was anxious that President Manuel Quezon hear of his progress. Quezon at that time lay dying of tuberculosis in a hospital in the United States. When he heard the news, Quezon gathered up his waning strength and said happily to his wife, "Aurora, he's only three hundred miles away!" The impossible had become possible.

Chapter 12

RETURN TO THE PHILIPPINES

W<small>HILE</small> MacArthur was carrying out his brilliant strategy in the Southwest Pacific, Admiral Nimitz was also busy in the Central Pacific area.

In November of 1943, Nimitz's forces took Tarawa in the Gilbert Islands. As a frontal assault, Tarawa proved costly to the Marines who came ashore. Another frontal assault resulted in the taking of Kwajalein atoll in the Marshall Islands on January 31, 1944. Nimitz's forces went on from here to Eniwetok. By mid-June his forces were on Saipan in the Marianas. This was followed by the Battle of the Philippine Seas, where Admiral Nimitz's naval forces clashed with the Japanese. At the end of the first day of this sea battle, the Japanese had lost two carriers and 402 carrier-based planes, while the Americans had lost only twenty-six planes. At the close of the two-day battle, the Japanese had lost four more aircraft carriers, as well as a battleship, a cruiser and a tanker.

There were other victories achieved by Admiral Nimitz, as, for example, over Tinian in the Marianas and over Guam. In fact, the progress of both General MacArthur and Admiral

Nimitz posed a major problem in the war's future strategy.

Sitting in Washington, the Joint Chiefs of Staff tried to decide where to move next in the Pacific. The Navy wanted to bypass the Philippines and move instead on Formosa by direct assault. From Formosa, they argued, they could acquire land bases on the mainland of China, only a short distance away. Then from both Formosa and China, the Allied air forces could bomb Japan. MacArthur considered this proposal a horror because the cost in lives in making such a frontal attack would be enormous. Instead, established as he was only a few hundred miles away from the Philippines, he believed that it was the duty of the United States to liberate its Commonwealth. He grew discouraged about the final decision when he received a message from General Marshall: "We must be careful not to allow our personal feeling and Philippine political considerations to overrule our great objective."

Weeks passed amid this uncertainty regarding the next move. But each rumor from Washington echoed the opinion that the Philippines would be bypassed. Then one day MacArthur received a confidential message. He was to proceed to Pearl Harbor in Hawaii by July 26, 1944, for a conference with a "Mr. Big."

When the *Bataan* braked to a stop on the Hawaiian runway, MacArthur learned immediately that "Mr. Big" was President Roosevelt. Although he favored the Navy's plan to bypass the Philippines, the President felt a lingering doubt and wanted to give both General MacArthur and Admiral Nimitz one last opportunity to explain their views.

MacArthur sensed that President Roosevelt had already made up his mind in favor of the Navy's proposal to proceed to Formosa. Yet he and the President greeted each other warmly and immediately fell into a talk about their early friendship during President Woodrow Wilson's administration. There was an inspection of the 25,000 soldiers on the field and MacArthur insisted that the weary President sit in his car while addressing the troops. Finally, after dinner in a mansion overlooking Waikiki Beach, MacArthur sat down with Roosevelt and Nimitz before a large wall map.

The President asked Admiral Nimitz to present his case first. Nimitz did so with skill. When the Admiral finished, MacArthur was even more sure that his own case was defeated before he spoke. Then the President called on MacArthur.

Slowly MacArthur rose, grasped the long pointer and walked determinedly to the wall map at the head of the room. He was at his eloquent best as he spoke softly but with deep feeling. He told of his admiration for Nimitz, but he said he had always opposed the costly frontal assault strategy employed by the Navy or by the Army in Europe. He pointed out that in two years of fighting he had lost fewer men than were killed in the single assault against Anzio in Italy. Then he presented the military case for capturing the Philippines instead of bypassing it. When he finished, he set the pointer down and returned to his seat. President Roosevelt then adjourned the meeting, and MacArthur felt that all was lost.

Afterward, the President requested MacArthur to visit him alone. At this meeting MacArthur outdid himself in eloquence as he presented the moral argument for returning to the Philippines. "Mr. President," he asked, "are you willing to accept responsibility for breaking a solemn promise to eighteen million Christian Filipinos that the Americans would return? Are you willing to bypass the Philippines and leave its millions of wards and thousands of American internees and prisoners of war to continue to languish in their agony and despair?"

With that, he rose to leave. As he neared the door, President Roosevelt suddenly called out, "Wait a minute, Douglas! Come back here."

MacArthur walked back. The President's face looked uncertain. Then he set his jaw and shook his head at MacArthur. "Well, Douglas, you win," he said. "But I'm going to have a heck of a time over this with that old bear, Ernie King!" (Admiral Ernest King was the President's chief naval adviser.)

Roosevelt then called in Admiral Nimitz, who took the decision well. He and MacArthur quickly worked up a target date of November 15 for a landing at Sarangani Bay, which lay near the bottom of the southern Philippine island of Mindanao.

MacArthur was elated with his success. He said of his farewell with the President, "We parted in a spirit of deep mutual regard. I knew then that I would never see him again." Roosevelt had spoken animatedly about his coming campaign for a fourth term, but MacArthur recognized that he was already in poor health.

Hardly had he returned from his meeting with "Mr. Big" when MacArthur received bad news from Washington. On August first, death had come to President Quezon. It had been MacArthur's ambition for more than two years to return Quezon to Manila as head of the government. Now this would never be. Quezon's position was assumed by Vice President Sergio Osmena, whom MacArthur had known for years. Osmena soon arrived from Washington to be on hand for the return to the Philippines.

Early in September, 1944, MacArthur moved his advance headquarters to Hollandia to plan the Philippine campaign.

Here he lived with several staff members in a house made by joining three Army-type prefabricated houses. The house stood on top of a high hill and presented a scene of breathtaking beauty. Before the war, the chief business of Hollandia had been the gathering of bird-of-paradise feathers. Now it swarmed with military men busily engaged in preparing for the approaching struggle for the Philippines. Their camps were built far up on the slopes of Cyclops, a 6,000-foot-high mountain to the north of a twenty-mile-long lake with inky blue water. Pouring out of Cyclops was a majestic 500-foot waterfall, and all about were deep ravines, sharply pointed hill peaks and mysterious jungles.

D-Day for plunging into Mindanao had been set for mid-November. However, the entire course of MacArthur's strategy was changed by a minor incident. General Kenney had begun bombing Davao, the strong Japanese center on Mindanao on September first, in an effort aimed at softening up that area. Then on the thirteenth, one of Admiral Halsey's fliers was shot down over Leyte, the next major Philippine island north of Mindanao.

Fortunately, Filipino guerrilla fighters saved him from being taken prisoner by the Japanese. They helped him to return to his squadron, but before they did they briefed him on Japanese strength on Leyte. Upon his return, he told about his briefing and what he had to say was startling. Compared with Mindanao, there were weaker Japanese forces on Leyte. Even more important, there were few Japanese planes based there.

MacArthur and Nimitz were quick to see the significance of his information. Instead of wasting lives in a landing on Mindanao, they would leapfrog over that island and land on Leyte. If all went well, their proposed timetable for re-taking the Philippines could be cut by three months.

MacArthur and his staff began working feverishly on the new program for invading Leyte. He looked years younger than sixty-four as he dreamily spoke of returning before too long to Manila and rescuing his old comrades whom he had been forced to leave behind on Bataan and Corregidor.

Carefully he set up radio contact with guerrillas on Leyte. Word was spread to Japanese agents that he would land on Mindanao and he looked with great satisfaction at the hectic Japanese efforts to strengthen Mindanao. While the Japanese on that island were convinced that General Kenney's heavy bombings were a prelude to invasion, the actual purpose was to ensure that Japanese planes from Mindanao would not interfere at Leyte. Kenney also destroyed two large oil refineries at Balikaan on Borneo where the Japanese were getting 80 per cent of their aviation gasoline.

As the build-up of his forces continued, MacArthur grew impatient. When Kenney pointed out that they were still short in ground troops and ships, MacArthur replied, "I tell you I'm going back there this fall if I have to paddle a canoe with you flying cover for me with that B-17 of yours." Even later when Admiral Nimitz provided him with two of his infantry divisions and the support of his carrier force, MacArthur still considered this a "shoestring" operation. But he was eager to begin the venture.

On October 16th, MacArthur boarded the cruiser *Nashville* for the invasion. Almost two million tons of equipment had been prepared for use in the weeks ahead. He walked the Admiral's deck, straining for a view of the land he had once fled. But it was not until the twentieth that the invasion fleet entered Leyte Gulf on the eastern side of the island.

Two divisions were to hit the beach at Dulag and two others near Tacloban a few miles away on the gulf. An aide walked into MacArthur's cabin while the General was preparing to land with the troops. He was dropping an old revolver in a pocket. "That belonged to my father," he explained. "I take it merely to insure that I'm not captured alive."

In a heavy downpour, MacArthur went ashore with the third assault wave at what was known as Red Beach. The small landing barge was swung over the side of the ship and continued in the water until it reached a point fifty yards from shore. The water was only knee-deep and he waded from there to the seared coral sand. Behind him came Colonel Carlos Romulo, who had run the radio station on Corregidor and had been the last man to escape from Bataan in 1942. Said Romulo: "There was the tall MacArthur, with the water reaching up to his knees, and behind him there was little Romulo, trying to keep his head above water."

This was the sacred moment for MacArthur, to stand again on Philippine soil. The troops were about three hundred yards inland on the long flat beach and were exchanging fire with Japanese soldiers hiding in pillboxes. MacArthur paid no attention to the snipers' bullets. He puffed on his corncob pipe and said to President Osmena, "Well, we're back as we promised in March, 1942."

He walked among his men who were lying on the ground behind the cover of trees during the sniping engagement. One soldier looked up and yelled to his buddy, "Hey, there's General MacArthur!"

The other continued looking for snipers. "Oh, yeah," he called back. "And I suppose he's got Eleanor Roosevelt with him!"

When MacArthur had first arrived in Australia in March,

1942, he had said, "I came through and I shall return." During those next few years those words had become a message of hope throughout the Philippines. Guerrilla bands had used his statement as indication that MacArthur was a man of his word and would one day return to liberate the islands. In radio broadcasts to the Philippines, these words were constantly repeated to keep up courage under the noses of the conquerors.

Now after two years, seven months and three days he had returned to fulfill his promise. A microphone had been set up on the beach, and, filled with emotion, MacArthur reported to the people of the Philippines. "I have returned," he began.

"By the grace of Almighty God our forces stand again on Philippine soil . . . soil consecrated in the blood of our two peoples. We have come dedicated and committed to the task of destroying every vestige of enemy control over your daily lives, and of restoring . . . the liberties of your people.

"At my side is your President, Sergio Osmena. . . . The seat of your government is now, therefore, firmly re-established on Philippine soil. . . . The hour of your redemption is here. . . . Rally to me. Let the indomitable spirit of Bataan and Corregidor lead on. As the lines of battle roll forward to bring you within the zone of operations, rise and strike. . . . For your homes and hearths, strike! For future generations of your sons and daughters, strike! In the name of your sacred dead, strike! Let no heart be faint. Let every arm be steeled. The guidance of Divine God points the way."

Chapter 13

CORREGIDOR REVISITED

O<small>NCE</small> his initial excitement at returning to the Philippines had passed, MacArthur looked ahead to the bitter task that lay before his men in liberating all of the islands.

The difficulties they would encounter became immediately obvious to him from the fanatic resistance put up by the Japanese forces on Leyte. Under the leadership of General Tomoyuki Yamashita, who had conquered Singapore and was also known as the "Tiger of Malaya," the 23,000 Japanese soldiers on Leyte fought as if the outcome of the entire war depended on them. In addition, the thousands upon thousands of Japanese reinforcements, who were landed on the western side of Leyte and rushed across the island to pin down MacArthur's men, were of the same sort.

Many organized themselves into suicide squadrons and threw themselves ferociously at the Americans. When newsmen questioned Colonel Romulo about the evident lack of speed on the part of the Americans in taking Leyte, Romulo turned to MacArthur for the answer. "Tell them that if I like I can finish Leyte in two weeks," said MacArthur. "But I won't! I have too great a responsibility to the mothers and wives in America. I will not take by sacrifice what I can achieve by strategy."

All the while MacArthur continued to walk about the front lines with his usual disregard for personal safety. And as always his good luck remained with him, though there were frequent close calls. On one occasion a Japanese tank suddenly came lumbering down the road toward him as he headed for Dulag. Fortunately, American artillery hit it with direct fire. When he and Kenney were inspecting the Japanese airdrome near Dulag, crossfire raged between soldiers of both sides. Worriedly, Kenney said to MacArthur, "I would feel much better if I were inspecting the place from an airplane." Later Kenney added, "I was glad when we finally decided to go back to the beach."

After a few days of heavy fighting, Tacloban, the capital of the province, was taken and MacArthur set up his advanced headquarters here. In a formal ceremony he restored to President Osmena his rightful constitutional powers over Leyte, even though he had only a toehold on the island.

Hardly had MacArthur moved into his headquarters building when a Japanese airplane swooped low over Tacloban and strafed the building. An aide ran into MacArthur's combination bedroom-office and found him calmly working at his desk. "Thank God, General!" he cried. "I thought you were killed."

Bullet holes were in the wall only a few inches above MacArthur's head. "I'm not dead yet," MacArthur passed off the incident. "But thank you for coming in."

Only four days after the successful landing, the entire Leyte campaign was suddenly in danger of total collapse. The Navy had been entrusted with the task of protecting the men on the beaches and in Leyte Gulf from the Japanese navy. Admiral

Kinkaid's Seventh Fleet was to protect western and southern entrances into Leyte Gulf. Admiral Halsey's Third Fleet was to guard the northern and eastern approaches. Halsey's crucial point to control was the San Bernardino Strait, which was the vital watery highway between Samar, the large island just above Leyte, and Luzon above Samar. As long as he bottled up the strait, a Japanese fleet coming down the western side of the Philippines could not cross over to the eastern side and slip into Leyte Gulf.

On the twenty-fourth of October, three large Japanese fleets were discovered steaming toward Leyte. One came from the south between Mindanao and Leyte and attempted to crash its way into Leyte Gulf through Surigao Strait that separated both islands. Kinkaid's ships went after this fleet and ambushed it so completely that only a single Japanese destroyer managed to escape.

A second Japanese fleet, known as the Japanese Central Force, under Admiral Kurita, had begun in the meantime to thread its way from the west toward the San Bernardino Strait. Reports to Admiral Halsey were that his own fliers had inflicted such heavy damage to the Japanese Central Force that it was no longer a menace.

Now came news of the third Japanese fleet, the Northern Force, coming down the eastern coast of Luzon toward Leyte. What Halsey did not know was that reports on the crippling of the Japanese Central Force were much exaggerated. In addition, the Northern Force was merely a decoy. It was a suicide squadron to lure him away from the San Bernardino Strait, so that the Central Fleet could pass through from the west and then race down to Leyte Gulf.

Jumping to the bait, Admiral Halsey moved his entire squadron northward to intercept the carriers of the Japanese

Northern Force. This left the San Bernardino Strait unguarded, and with speed Admiral Kurita slipped through and headed for Leyte Gulf. With his fleet of four swift battleships, six heavy cruisers, two light cruisers and eleven destroyers, Kurita faced only light opposition as he sped toward his objective. What lay in his path was an outnumbered and outgunned force of smaller American ships.

When MacArthur learned of Admiral Kurita's advancing fleet, he realized the horror of what lay in store for his unprotected soldiers. "Probably two hundred or more of our vessels were exposed in the Bay of Tacloban," he said. "The enemy's heavy guns would have experienced little trouble in pounding the remaining transports and landing craft. Shore positions and troops installations could have been bombarded almost at leisure."

He sent several messages to Admiral Nimitz at Pearl Harbor to order Halsey's return. Frantically, Nimitz tried to reach Halsey, who was by now 300 miles away. But the radio messages failed to reach Halsey. Several small American ships bravely gave battle to Kurita's fleet in an effort to buy time, and many were sunk. At fearful odds, American planes also went out to meet the challenge. Said MacArthur, "The planes were practically destroyed and my potential air umbrella to protect my ground forces and operations disappeared." At one point, after failing to reach Halsey because of radio interference, Nimitz sent him the following mesage: "The whole world wants to know where is Task Force 34!"

Then a miracle happened. Just as the situation had almost grown hopeless, Admiral Kurita suddenly ordered his ships to stop firing and to head north away from Leyte Gulf. "He was unaware of the true battle situation," said MacArthur thankfully. Had he "proceeded into Leyte Gulf, the American invasion would in all probability have experienced a setback of incalculable proportions."

By the grace of this miracle in the Battle of Leyte Gulf, MacArthur could turn once more to the task of liberating Leyte. In early December he was able to act with characteristic strategy. Far around the island on the west side of Leyte his men made a surprise amphibious landing at Ormoc. Moving quickly ahead, they struck at General Yamashita's army from the rear. Then after seizing the center of the Yamashita Line, they split the Japanese army in two and trapped each section. On December 26th, all organized resistance ended on Leyte.

Southwest of Luzon lay the large island of Mindoro. This became MacArthur's next target because its airfields would provide him cover for his final advance, which would be on Luzon.

MacArthur's strategy was to go up the east coast of Mindoro. This created the impression that he planned to land on the southern coast of Luzon and then work his way northward to Manila. Reacting to his ruse, the Japanese rushed two divisions from northern Luzon to Bataan and the town of Batangas in the south of that island. This was exactly what MacArthur desired, for his strategy was to land at Lingayen Gulf about 110 miles north of Manila and proceed *down* the island of Luzon instead of up. Then, when the Japanese turned their Luzon army of 235,000 to meet the threat from Lingayen Gulf, he would land another army on the southern coast. "Both forces ashore, with but minor loss," he said, "will then close like a vise on the enemy deprived of supplies and destroy him."

When MacArthur set January 9, 1945, for the landing at Lingayen Gulf, members of his staff disagreed with this target date. Some claimed that they lacked enough time to prepare for the drive. Others pointed out that Admiral Nimitz had asked for the return of a hundred transports he had lent MacArthur. Nevertheless, MacArthur would not change his mind. On a clear day he could see Manila from Mindoro and he would no longer put off this final drive to liberate all of the Philippines.

MacArthur had been made a five-star General of the Army on December 18, 1944. Now, on January fifth, as he boarded the cruiser *Boise* for the Lingayen Gulf landing, a five-star ensign flew from the mast. At dawn on the ninth, large naval vessels bombarded the landing beaches on the gulf, and shortly after nine A.M. the first G. I.'s raced toward shore. By dark, almost 70,000 men were safely ashore.

MacArthur had no fixed timetable for the campaign down the central plains of Luzon between the mountains to Bataan, Corregidor and Manila. This would be up to General Krueger and his Sixth Army.

However, MacArthur had a personal reason for speed. At Santo Tomas University and at Bilibid, near Manila, at Los Baños on Laguna de Bay and at Pangatian near Cabanatuan were thousands of military and civilian prisoners of war. He was told that when news of the landing reached those prisons, guards had become brutal. Unless he could liberate the inmates soon, they would all die.

Though he did not press General Krueger to move more swiftly than safety permitted, he himself moved recklessly toward Manila. At one time he was fifty miles closer to Manila than was Krueger. General Kenney came to visit him at his advanced headquarters at San Miguel. Kenney was shocked to find the General looking exhausted. Nevertheless, MacArthur insisted on discussing military problems long after midnight. When Kenney rose before dawn and told an officer that he had to leave without saying good-by, the reply was that MacArthur had left for the front two hours earlier.

It was obvious to MacArthur that the Army would not be able to brush aside the heavy Japanese resistance and reach the prisoners of war before it was too late. Something daring must be attempted. Quickly he dispatched 134 hand-picked Rangers to take the prison near Cabanatuan, deep inside Japanese lines. Here were 500 prisoners of war who had served with him on Bataan and Corregidor.

Under cover of darkness, the Rangers reached the prison and with complete surprise they overpowered 200 Japanese guards. MacArthur met the prisoners at the town of Guimba. All looked like skeletons. Throughout the war, the Japanese had dinned into them that MacArthur had deserted them. But they felt only warmth toward him as he walked through their ranks, his face tear-stained as he remembered almost all of them by name.

With this one prison freed, MacArthur wanted the other prisoners saved. He called in Major General Verne Mudge. "Get to Manila!" he ordered. "Go around the Japs, bounce off the Japs. But get to Manila! Free the 3,500 internees at Santo Tomas. Take Malacanan Palace and the Legislative Building!"

Mudge took along a brave crew of two squadrons and four days' supplies. They sped all the way on their 100-mile dash to Manila. Along the way, they had to swim rivers, charge machine-gun nests and engage in hand-to-hand combat. Onward they pressed with almost no sleep. On the third day they reached Manila as night fell. By eight-thirty, they crashed through the gates of the university compound and freed the prisoners.

In February, the Bataan Peninsula was retaken. Then, on March second, MacArthur solemnly stepped ashore on Corregidor. He had travel by PT boat, just as he had once left the island, and he brought with him the staff members who had gone with him from the Rock to Australia in March, 1942. "This visit is easing an ache that has been in my heart for three years," he said. He walked along lost in thought over his former scene of torment. An American flag went up on a battered flagpole and he said: "I see the old flagstaff still stands. Haul the colors to its peak and let no enemy ever haul them down."

MacArthur had hoped to take Manila without destruction. However, the Japanese had fortified the city and bitter hand-to-hand fighting lasted almost a month. More than 2,500 Japanese fought to the death within the ancient walled part of the city called Intramuros. It was not until March fourth that the last Japanese soldier gave up. Even before then MacArthur held a formal ceremony at Malacanan Palace where he turned over full constitutional powers to Filipino leaders.

He sent for his wife and son to come to Manila. Their former penthouse apartment atop the Manila Hotel was in ruins. He found the burned-out grand piano and the charred remains of his fine library and scrapbooks. His reaction was to shrug his shoulders. "On to Tokyo!" he said to newsmen

Chapter 14

SURRENDER ON THE *MISSOURI*

Events piled high upon events before General MacArthur was able to declare on August 11, 1945, that all the islands of the Philippines were liberated. President Roosevelt had died on April 12th and was succeeded by his Vice President, Harry S. Truman, of Independence, Missouri. In Europe, MacArthur's former aide, General Eisenhower, had brought the war in that theater to a successful conclusion with the surrender of Nazi Germany on May 8th.

The war with Japan was still not finished. On February 19, Admiral Nimitz's forces invaded the small, volcanic-ash-covered island of Iwo Jima. This was far to the northeast of the Philippines and south of the islands of Japan. Nimitz hoped to use Iwo Jima as an advanced airfield to provide tactical air support for troops invading Japan. The enemy had 20,000 troops on Iwo who fought so fiercely that by March 16th, when the Marines conquered the island, the American casualties in dead and wounded totaled almost 24,000 men. Then in March began the Okinawa campaign to take the island below Kyushu, the Japanese island at the bottom of its homeland empire. This also proved costly, for American casualties totaled about 40,000.

All during that spring of 1945, Japan proper was subjected to a steady pounding from the air to prepare for an invasion. B-29's flying from the Marianas were over Japan on an average of 1,400 planes a week. Admiral Halsey's Third Fleet roamed through Japanese coastal waters and shelled towns and cities.

Nevertheless, MacArthur knew from intelligence reports that an actual invasion of Japan might prove costly. Japanese on the mainland islands were feverishly digging caves and tunnels behind the beaches and storing food and ammunition for last-ditch stands. Kamikaze suicide planes lay camouflaged on airfields throughout Japan. Despite the battering she was being subjected to, Japan still had more than 2,500,000 soldiers on her homeland bases and a million more reinforcements in Manchuria.

One of the last acts of President Roosevelt had been his announcement that there would be a split command for the actual invasion. MacArthur would direct the Army forces, while Nimitz would be in charge of naval operations. Later, from the Joint Chiefs of Staff in Washington, came the target dates. The entire invasion was to be known as "Downfall," and was to consist of two operations. The first was "Olympic," an assault on the south island of Kyushu on November first. Then on March 1, 1946, would come "Coronet," or the invasion of Honshu with the national capital of Tokyo.

MacArthur worked hard on "Downfall" plans, though he permitted himself one diversion. It was in June when he went ashore with the assault wave of Australian troops under his command to capture Borneo and put a stop to that island's oil shipments to Japan.

Again his staff officers pleaded with him not to expose

himself to the heavy fire of the enemy. And as usual, he refused. A press photographer just in front of him was felled by a sniper's bullet. Another time he was so far ahead of the advanced Australian unit that its general, Sir Leslie Morshead, shook his head and said, "This is the first time I have ever heard of a commander in chief acting as the point."

Near Balikpapan on Borneo's east coast, he was studying a map with other officers atop a hill when an enemy machine gun began firing at them. Said an aide, "Bullets whined about us, spurts of dust were kicked into the air." After a while, MacArthur folded the map and suggested that the men go over to another hill and see what was going on. As they started down the hill, MacArthur said, "By the way, I think it would be a good idea to have a patrol take out that machine gun before someone gets hurt."

By August, MacArthur was well into the problems of Operation Olympic. He had already assigned General Krueger and his Sixth Army to the task of assaulting Kyushu when suddenly there was no need for invading the enemy's homeland. On August 6th, an atomic bomb exploded on Hiroshima. When the Japanese government did not surrender, another A-bomb fell on the industrial center of Nagasaki. Finally, on August 13th, Emperor Hirohito spoke by radio transcript to his people. He told his subjects that they had lost the war and "hostilities cease forthwith." He and his government would be subject to the orders of the Supreme Commander of the Allied Powers.

The following day President Truman accepted "the unconditional surrender of Japan." For some time President Truman had pondered over the question of who should direct the occupation of Japan. Some of his advisers had suggested Admiral Nimitz, while others suggested General MacArthur.

Acting with speed now, he won agreement from the British, Chinese and Soviet governments that General MacArthur be appointed "Supreme Commander for the Allied Powers," or SCAP, as the occupation administration would be called.

As a man of war, MacArthur had to adapt his thinking to peace. But first must come the actual surrender of Japan. As soon as he heard of his appointment, he ordered Japanese representatives to fly to Manila for instructions on the surrender. He told the group to paint green crosses on their plane, and then, to cap his own early defeat and later victory, insisted that they use the call letters B-A-T-A-A-N.

At first the Japanese representatives stalled. They pretended not to understand his instructions. Then they asked permission to use the call letters J-N-P instead of B-A-T-A-A-N. "The letters are B-A-T-A-A-N," MacArthur curtly replied.

The sixteen-man Japanese delegation finally left Tokyo on August 19th. When they arrived in Manila, MacArthur would not see them. However, his staff aides informed them fully about the actual surrender process. One order was to repair Atsugi Airfield outside of Yokohama for the early arrival of MacArthur. General Kenney had selected Atsugi because its runways were long. In addition, it was not only near Yokohama but it was also only thirty miles from Tokyo. Other instructions were to provide transportation from Atsugi Airfield to Yokohama, turn over the New Grand Hotel there to MacArthur and his men, remove all propellers from Japanese planes on Atsugi, and to withdraw all troops from the Tokyo Bay area. The official surrender was to take place aboard the battleship *Missouri* in Tokyo Bay.

Later, when the Japanese delegation departed, MacArthur announced he planned to land at Atsugi on August 28th.

This gave his staff about a week to work out the details. Many were concerned about his setting foot in the territory of a people who had considered him their chief enemy for more than three years. With 2,500,000 fanatic soldiers roaming Japan, there was every indication that a few at least would attempt to assassinate MacArthur. However, MacArthur considered his going to Japan at the outset of the occupation as a necessary gamble. Besides, he was familiar with Orientals. He knew from his many tours of duty in the Philippines and from his one military stay in Japan, early in the century, that the Japanese national spirit was one of traditional chivalry, encompassed in the philosophy known as *Bushido.*

With this in mind, he gave no thought to possible danger to himself in Japan. He was therefore surprised when he was told what Churchill's comment had been: "Of all the amazing deeds of bravery of the war, I regard MacArthur's personal landing at Atsugi as the greatest of the lot."

When the Japanese reported they were having a little trouble repairing Atsugi Airfield, MacArthur postponed his trip two days. Fear spread throughout MacArthur's staff when they learned the reason for the trouble at Atsugi. It was at this airfield that kamikaze pilots were trained and based. When word reached them of the impending surrender, they refused to accept this situation. First they dropped leaflets over Tokyo which denounced the advisers of Emperor Hirohito. Then they staged a wild revolt and even tried to seize the palace grounds. Just before MacArthur's expected arrival, they were finally subdued, but not before they had burned and machine-gunned the residences of the Prime Minister and the President of the Privy Council.

As MacArthur made last-minute preparations to leave the

Philippines, that government paid him high honors. First he was awarded honorary citizenship in the Philippines. A second resolution said that his name would be carried forever "on the company rolls of the Philippine Army, and at parade roll calls, when his name is called, the senior noncommissioned officer shall answer 'Present in spirit.'" Coins and stamps in his honor were to bear the inscription: DEFENDER—LIBERATOR.

It was at two P.M. on August 30 when a C-4 with the word BATAAN printed on its nose circled Atsugi Airfield and bounced to a poor landing on the runway. MacArthur stepped out, his corncob pipe in his hand. Then he grinned at General Eichelberger and told him, "Bob, this is the pay-off."

Fifteen Japanese divisions in that area had not yet been disarmed. MacArthur's top generals had warily slipped pistols into their shoulder holsters. "Leave them behind," he ordered. "Those pistols won't do much good if the Japanese don't really mean what they said about surrendering." Afterward, a number of Japanese told General Kenney that "the sight of all those generals and officers of MacArthur's staff walking around unarmed, in a country of seventy million people who only a few days before were enemies, made a tremendous impression on the Japanese."

The Japanese had sent old, worn-out cars to carry MacArthur and his staff into Yokohama. Along the route into the city, 30,000 Japanese soldiers lined both sides of the highway, their backs to MacArthur as they kept close watch on the Japanese who had come for a look at their conquerors. All this protection was unnecessary, as MacArthur knew, from his understanding of Japanese character.

Yokohama streets were deserted as MacArthur and his

aides rode through the bombed-out city to the New Grand Hotel. This was one of the few buildings still standing after six months of B-29 raids that had battered this city of one million people. One of MacArthur's first orders after learning of the severe food shortages in Yokohama and other Japanese cities was to bar all occupation forces from consuming local food. This immediately added to his reputation as a generous conqueror.

MacArthur was busily at work on the final details for the surrender when word came to him that General "Skinny" Wainwright, whom he left in charge on Corregidor in 1942, had been freed from a Japanese prison camp near Mukden. Also liberated from that same camp was General Sir Arthur E. Percival, who had commanded British forces at Singapore. He immediately ordered that the two be flown to Atsugi.

Wainwright walked in leaning on a cane. He looked like a skeleton. At the sight of him, MacArthur threw his arms around him, but was so overcome with emotion that he could not talk. Wainwright fumbled for words. He believed that because he had surrendered on Corregidor the Army would not accept him back. "Why, Jim," MacArthur comforted him, "you can have command of a corps whenever you want it!"

The surrender was to take place on Sunday morning, September second, aboard Admiral Halsey's Third Fleet flagship, the U.S.S. *Missouri*. MacArthur had insisted that Wainwright and Percival be his honor guests at the ceremony.

At 8:45 that foggy morning, MacArthur went out by destroyer to Halsey's ship. A few minutes later Japanese Foreign Minister Mamoru Shigemitsu, who had a wooden leg, hobbled nervously aboard. He was followed by his fellow delegate, General Yoshijiro Umezu of the Imperial General

Staff, and nine aides. Prince Shigemitsu and two of his three
civilian aides wore top hats, frock coats and striped trousers.
General Kenney said that the seven Japanese military men
present wore ragged, unpressed uniforms, probably to show
that they considered the proceedings of little consequence to
them. "I believe that I disliked them that day more than at
any time during the war," he said. "They didn't know how to
lose gracefully."

For the occasion, MacArthur had invited generals and
admirals of all Allies. These men now lined the veranda
deck of Halsey's ship three deep. In the center of the deck
stood a table and on it in readiness lay the white surrender
documents. MacArthur had seen to it that the American flag
that flew over the *Missouri* that morning was the same flag
that had flown on December 7, 1941, over the Capitol Building in Washington, D. C. "We waited a few minutes, standing in the public gaze like penitent boys awaiting the dreaded
schoolmaster," said one of Prince Shigemitsu's aides.

Then MacArthur strode to a microphone on the other
side of the table from the Japanese. He wore an open-neck
shirt and his lucky gold-braided cap and his hand trembled
slightly as the significance of the occasion suddenly came
over him.

"We are gathered here, representatives of the major war-
ring powers," he began, "to conclude a solemn agreement
whereby peace may be restored. The issues, involving diver-
gent ideals and ideologies, have been determined on the
battlefields of the world and hence are not for our discussion or debate. . . .

"It is my earnest hope and indeed the hope of all mankind
that from this solemn occasion a better world shall emerge
out of the blood and carnage of the past—a world founded

upon faith and understanding—a world dedicated to the dignity of man and the fulfillment of his most cherished wish —for freedom, tolerance and justice."

He concluded firmly with, "I now invite the representatives of the Emperor of Japan and the Japanese Government and the Japanese Imperial Staff Headquarters to sign the instrument of surrender at the places indicated."

Prince Shigemitsu limped to the table and sat down to sign his name first. He was so nervous that he had trouble getting his wooden leg under the table. First he removed his tall silk hat, then his gloves. Next he put his hat back on his head, removed it once more and finally dropped both hat and gloves on the table. When he fumbled in his search for the line on which he was to sign his name, MacArthur grew impatient. "Sutherland!" he called sternly to his Chief of Staff. "Show him where to sign!"

After General Umezu signed, MacArthur called on Wainwright and Percival to stand behind him while he signed his name as Supreme Commander. He used five pens to complete his signature. One went to Wainwright, a second to Percival, the third to President Truman, the fourth to the *Missouri,* and the last for himself. The fifth pen was a cheap one that belonged to his wife.

After MacArthur came Admiral Nimitz who, with Halsey as his witness, signed for the United States. Then came signatures from the representatives of China, Great Britain, the Soviet Union, France, Australia, Canada, and New Zealand.

Following the signing, MacArthur spoke briefly by radio to the people of the United States. He said: "Today the guns are silent. A great tragedy has ended. A great victory has been won. . . . The entire world lies quietly at peace. . . .

And in reporting this to you, the people, I speak for the thousands of silent lips, forever stilled among the jungles and the beaches and in the deep waters of the Pacific which marked the way. I speak for the unnamed brave millions homeward bound to take up the challenge of the future which they did so much to salvage from the brink of disaster."

The entire proceedings lasted only eighteen minutes. Just as the meeting broke up, the sky was suddenly darkened by a powerful display of American air power. Across the heavens flew a thousand B-29 Superfortresses and a thousand Navy fighters and dive bombers. On they flew toward the sacred snowcapped mountains of Fujiyama.

These seemed so unnecessary now that peace had come to the world.

Chapter 15

RULER OF JAPAN

Fᴏʟʟᴏᴡɪɴɢ the surrender of Japan, General Mac-Arthur took on an entirely new role in his life. From a military leader, dedicated to the defeat of the enemy, he was now to change to a statesman to help a feudal Japan become a democratic nation.

There was nothing in the directive under which he was to operate to give an inkling of this. To the contrary, its philosophy was one of tight military control over the former enemy. Said the directive of August 14, 1945: "From the moment of surrender, the authority of the Emperor and the Japanese Government to rule the state will be subject to you and you will take such steps as you deem proper to effectuate the surrender terms. You will exercise supreme command over all land, sea and air forces which may be allocated for enforcement in Japan of the surrender terms by the Allied forces concerned."

However, even before MacArthur arrived in Japan for the surrender in Tokyo Bay, he had jotted down some of the basic things he hoped to accomplish as Supreme Commander of the occupation.

These goals were: "First destroy the military power...
then build the structure of representative government. . . .
Enfranchise the women. . . . Free the political prisoners. . . . Liberate the farmers. . . . Establish a free labor
movement. . . . Encourage a free economy. . . . Abolish
police oppression. . . . Develop a free and responsible
press. . . . Liberalize education. . . . Decentralize the political power."

Shortly after the surrender, MacArthur spoke of his occupation philosophy to the Allied Council for Japan, which
consisted of representatives of the victorious nations. "May
we as victors," he said, "become architects of a new Japan—
a Japan reoriented to peace, security and justice. . . . Were
we but to ensure the thoroughness of Japan's defeat, then
leave it prostrate in the ashes of total collapse, history would
point to a task poorly done. . . . It is for us now to guide
its people to rededicate themselves to higher principles, ideals
and purposes... that they firmly may meet the challenge
to future utility in the service of mankind."

No one was better suited than he to take on this task
because of his knowledge of the workings of the Oriental
mind. For instance, on the battlefield MacArthur found that
it helped troop morale to expose himself to the same dangers
they underwent. He was the "Old Man" who waded onto
beaches in island assaults. He visited camps, talked to his men
and puffed on his corncob pipe.

MacArthur realized that the Japanese would soon lose their
awe and then their respect for him if he mingled freely with
them. They wanted the mystery of an aloof ruler who was
seldom seen and never lingered. The result was that he pur-
posely maintained himself as a solemn-faced unapproachable
person so far as the Japanese public was concerned.

To keep up this picture, he made the superb American Embassy the home for himself, his wife and seven-year-old Arthur. His office was on the sixth floor of the impressive Dai-Ichi Building in the heart of Tokyo, across the way from the Palace grounds. In Japanese "Dai-Ichi" means "Number One." Tall, handsome sentries, smartly uniformed, stood at stiff attention outside both the Embassy and SCAP headquarters.

Each morning, MacArthur arose at seven, donned his dressing gown on which had been sewn the large black "A" he had won at West Point for baseball. After breakfast, he worked until ten-thirty when a shiny black Cadillac pulled into the Embassy's driveway. A large crowd of Japanese gathered across the street each morning to watch him enter his car. Another crowd waited at the Dai-Ichi Building to stare at him while he entered SCAP headquarters. This scene was repeated when he returned to the Embassy for lunch and when he went back to his office again afterward. For six years he kept to this narrow routine and was not otherwise seen in public.

At the same time that MacArthur maintained his aloofness, he made a point to treat individual Japanese, no matter what their station, with simple kindness. For instance, the day after he moved into the Dai-Ichi Building, he strode into the elevator and found a Japanese carpenter inside. In great embarrassment, the man excused himself and left the elevator. MacArthur insisted that they ride up together.

Not long afterward MacArthur received the following letter: "I am the humble carpenter whom last week you not only permitted but insisted ride with you on the same elevator. I have reflected on this act of courtesy and I realize that no Japanese general would have done as you did."

Throughout his six-year stay in Japan as Supreme Allied Commander, MacArthur held to a working schedule of seven days a week. Generally, he did not leave his office before eight P.M. Each day was a hard one, with policy to make, hundreds of letters to read and several visitors to interview. One Sunday evening he turned to an aide and asked what time it was. The reply was "Ten-thirty." MacArthur stood up and a wry grin crossed his face. "What do you say we take the rest of the weekend off?" he asked.

When MacArthur assumed command over Japan, he realized the enormous task that lay before him. "Never in history has a nation and its people been more completely crushed than were the Japanese at the end of the struggle," he said. "They had suffered more than a military debacle. Their entire faith in the Japanese way of life, cherished as invincible for many centuries, perished in the agony of their total defeat."

The country lay in ruins. Not a smiling face could be seen. Everywhere there was a great shortage of food and millions were without work. This was fertile ground for communism unless MacArthur could awaken the shell-shocked nation and set its course wisely and on a firm foundation. While the people of Japan were trying to discover how their new Supreme Commander would treat them, MacArthur showed his intentions by pouring American flour and food staples into Japan for local relief.

As a military conqueror, there were several things Mac-Arthur had to do before he could embark on his program to democratize Japan. His first official act was to liberate all Allied prisoners held by Japan in the territories she had previously captured. Another order demobilized and disarmed four million Japanese soldiers and sailors. He also decreed that Japanese nationals overseas were to return to Japan. Within a year and a half about six million came home. Then he ordered war criminals brought to trial.

From the start, MacArthur had trouble with some of the representatives of the other Allied nations who insisted that Emperor Hirohito be tried as a war criminal. Fortunately, MacArthur, who had a keen grasp of what the Emperor meant to his people, was above the veto power of the Allied countries. He realized that the Emperor was the spiritual leader of Japan, and as such could be utilized to give Mac-Arthur's rulings the force of authority. Had the Emperor been placed on trial his people would have immediately grown bitter and noncooperative. "Without the Emperor," said MacArthur, "we would have needed a force of two million men." With the Emperor's person untouched, the occupation forces never totaled more than two hundred thousand.

Nevertheless, MacArthur also realized that to permit the Emperor to keep his absolute powers would defeat any attempts to democratize Japan. Not long after the Occupation began, MacArthur ordered the Emperor to come to the American Embassy for a talk. Although this proved an initial shock to the Japanese, its deeper meaning was that their ruler was just as subject to MacArthur as they were.

In November, 1945, MacArthur took a major step in diminishing the Emperor's authority by abolishing state Shinto. This was the state-controlled religion based on mythology, legend and paganism. Shintoism taught that the Emperor was the Son of Heaven and was divine; that all previous Emperors were gods; and that they, the empire and the Japanese people were also of divine origin. Furthermore, Shinto taught that one day Japan would rule the world and the highest purpose of every Japanese was to die in the service of his Emperor. This state-enforced religion had been used primarily by militarists to further their own goals of conquest.

The final blow to the Emperor's exalted position came on New Year's Day of 1946. On that day, Hirohito spoke over the radio and told his people he was not divine. Some of MacArthur's aides said that the language of the talk showed that MacArthur had written the Emperor's speech.

In his radio address, the Emperor made the following remarks: "The ties between us and our people do not depend upon mere legends and myths. They are not predicated on the false conception that the Emperor is divine and that the Japanese people are superior to other races and fated to rule the world."

With this death blow to state Shinto, MacArthur tackled other aspects of dictatorial control over the people of Japan. One such basic reform he accomplished was to abolish thought control and the Kempei-Tai, or secret police. An average of 20,000 persons a year had been jailed for expressing "dangerous thoughts." The Kempei-Tai had a spy organization operating from Tokyo that went into every home to frighten citizens from expressing any opinions that did not agree entirely with the militarists. Even those who said nothing but were considered to harbor "disloyal" thoughts were imprisoned. This extended even to members of the Cabinet.

Besides abolishing the Kempei-Tai, MacArthur also outlawed the Black Dragon and other secret societies whose basic activity was to promote militarism and the police state. From now on, said MacArthur, any person had the right to express himself freely without fear of punishment. Not only did he order the release of political prisoners but he also introduced the writ of habeas corpus, just as his father had done in the Philippines in 1901. People were no longer to be arrested without cause, but must be taken before a court to determine whether they were being held legally. In addition, MacArthur changed the entire character of the local police. Before, they had been notoriously harsh and unmerciful. Now, upon direct orders, they were made to understand that they were the servants and not the masters of the people.

Once he broke the chains and made possible the growth of political democracy in Japan, MacArthur determined that the Japanese people themselves must develop their own democratic institutions. "Democracy cannot be imposed upon a nation," he said. "It must have its origin in the understanding and faith of the common people."

His own role, he believed, was to suggest and prod, rather than to force. For instance, he realized that the grass roots of democracy lay in the towns and villages and not in the national government. It was essential, he said, that the people in every locality "be given complete freedom to express their will, and by assuming full responsibility to learn procedures of democratic government." Such experience locally would develop new leaders both for the towns and the nation.

There was no such thing as the right of local self-government when MacArthur came to Japan. There was instead complete control by the central government. Though he might have ordered the establishment of local freely elected governments, he knew well that it could survive only if done by the Japanese themselves. With this in mind, he first suggested and then successfully prodded the Diet (Japan's Parliament) to pass such a law. It stated that "local public entities shall have the right to manage their property affairs and administration and to enact their own regulations within the law."

Almost from the day he took charge, MacArthur pressed for a new constitution under which the nation would operate. The old constitution had come down from the Meiji reign of long ago and was nothing more than an antique document that imposed feudalism on the country.

At MacArthur's insistence, a committee of Japanese leaders was formed to revise the constitution and the people of Japan were invited to make suggestions. However, the committee stalled for four months, though it pretended to be hard at work. Finally, it produced a draft that did little to change the existing order. As in the Meiji constitution, the Emperor's powers were still absolute. Not only was he above all laws but none could be passed without his approval. Japan would still be ruled by a dictatorship.

It was now the beginning of February, 1946, and Mac-Arthur had ordered the first free election in Japanese history to take place in April. It was his hope that the voters would have the opportunity to express their opinions of a new constitution. He had suggested and prodded; now it was time for action.

First he ordered SCAP political experts to prepare a draft constitution based on his own principles. When the task was completed by mid-February, he asked that the draft be considered by the special Japanese committee. But again the committee stalled before expressing its dislike for promoting democracy in Japan. Said its chairman, "Some of the roses of the West, when cultivated in Japan, lose their fragrance."

MacArthur had had enough. He called the committee to meet with his staff nonstop around-the-clock until both sides agreed to a single draft. This meeting lasted almost forty-eight hours. Finally, late on March 5th, MacArthur accepted the compromise with these words: "The Japanese people thus turn their backs firmly upon the mysticism and unreality of the past and face instead a future of realism with a new faith and a new hope."

Every political party except the Communists eagerly accepted the blueprint of political democracy. In April, the voters supported those candidates who spoke out most firmly for the new constitution. Later, the Diet debated the document section by section for three months before passing it.

The constitution opened up an entirely new political existence for the Japanese. The Emperor was reduced to a figurehead with no political power. In turn, the authority of the Diet was strengthened. A bill of rights guaranteed freedom of speech, assembly, press, and religion. A unique feature was one in which Japan renounced war and the maintenance of an army.

MacArthur acted independently as Supreme Commander to give Japanese women the right to vote. So-called experts on Japan insisted that this was most unwise. They pointed out that the Japanese way of life made women the servants of men. By tradition and centuries of practice, women were forbidden to give thought to anything except household duties.

MacArthur calmly smiled and ignored the experts. Forty million women had to be liberated so that their voices could be heard in the new Japan. To maintain them in their form of slavery would only serve to deprive the country of vital brain power and their humane qualities.

Experience proved that MacArthur was entirely right. No other reform "had such heartwarming results," said one of his chief aides. In the very first election, more than thirteen

million women voted and more than thirty-five won election
to the Diet. These women legislators played a vital role in
improving working conditions, education and health legislation. Even more important, the right to vote emancipated
women in all regards. For the first time they entered business
and the professions, spoke out on issues and attained equal
status with men.

MacArthur was well aware that political democracy with
its freedom for the individual was greatly dependent on
economic freedom. It did a man little good to have the right
to disagree with government activities if he had no rights
regarding the way he earned his living.

For example, ten family clans, called Zaibatsu families,
owned 90 per cent of Japan's industries. They were so powerful financially that they prevented the development of competition from others. They forced many of their workers to
live inside their plants and treated them like slaves.

MacArthur lost little time ordering the Zaibatsu holdings
dissolved. The stock in their firms was taken from them at
cost and sold to the public and none of the Zaibatsu was
permitted to buy back any of the property. In the past, the
Zaibatsu clans had enjoyed a "tax-exempt" status. Now they
were required to pay taxes like everyone else. MacArthur
hoped by these moves to develop a competitive free enter-
prise system in Japan instead of monopoly.

As for the workers, MacArthur insisted that they be given
the right to organize for the first time into labor unions
and to bargain collectively with employers on wages, hours,
factory safety and other related matters. Within a year after
the Diet approved such a law, more than four million workers
organized themselves into 17,000 unions.

On the land, most farmers were peasants who spent their

lives as tenants and sharecroppers on large estates. Here land-lords took such a large part of their production as rent that they were in reality slaves. MacArthur considered their status to be degrading.

In place of their miserable existence, he prodded the Diet to pass laws giving them title to the property they worked with little personal gain. This was done by having the government buy the land from the owners and then sell it to the individual farm workers with payments stretching over twenty-five years. Within a few years, this program was so successful that 90 per cent of Japan's farmland was owned by those who worked it. MacArthur proudly hailed it as "the most successful experiment of its kind in history."

MacArthur moved in many other directions to spread democracy. One of his major programs was to reform the school system. Existing schoolbooks were filled with military propaganda. These were thrown out and replaced with hundreds of millions of textbooks that had no such purpose. He also promoted Romaji, or Roman letters, to replace picture writing or ideographs, with the result that the illiteracy rate dramatically decreased. There were about 60,000 characters in picture writing, each of which had to be memorized. They were so difficult to memorize that an average man could understand only a few thousand characters.

By 1950, MacArthur had successfully accomplished a democratic revolution in Japan. Coming in as a conqueror, he might have gained the reputation of a tyrant. Instead, he was the most beloved figure in Japan.

He was seventy that year, long past the age when most men retire. He had served his country long and well. Few had accomplished so much in a lifetime in his nation's entire history.

There was some talk that soon he would be going home. His son Arthur was twelve now and had never stepped foot on the soil of his native country.

However, in 1950, MacArthur was destined to return again to the battlefield. This time it was to be a peninsula on the mainland of Asia—Korea.

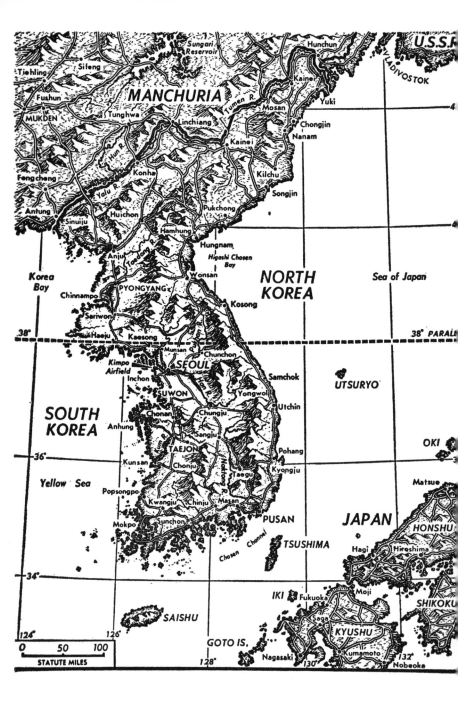

Chapter 16

BATTLE FOR KOREA

In all the time MacArthur served as Supreme Commander of Allied Powers in Japan, he made only two trips outside that country. The first was on July 4, 1946, when he traveled to Manila as the guest of honor at the Philippine Independence Day ceremonies. The Philippines were now at last an independent nation and MacArthur told Carlos Romulo, who was to represent the new country at the United Nations: "Today we have buried imperialism in the Orient."

MacArthur's other trip was to Korea in August, 1948. He had come to Seoul to attend the inauguration ceremony of the Republic of South Korea. The peninsula of Korea, jutting out from the mainland of Asia like a thumb pointing south at the islands of Japan, had fallen to Japan as a prize following the Russo-Japanese War of 1904. The name Korea meant "Land of the Morning Calm." However, Japan maintained tense control of her thirty million people and 85,000 square miles until her defeat in World War II.

One of the decisions of the victorious Allies was to liberate Korea and make her a free nation again. At the close of the war, American troops would accept the surrender of

Japanese forces in Korea up to the Thirty-eighth Parallel of North Latitude, while the Russians would accept the surrender above that artificial line. Afterward, arrangements were to be made to turn over both parts of Korea to a single government of their own choice.

Unfortunately, the Russians turned North Korea into an armed Communist stronghold. They would not agree to a free election because North Korea had a population only half as large as the twenty million in the south below the Thirty-eighth Parallel. Furthermore, they intended that southern Korea should fall to the North Korean Reds either through propaganda or invasion. As the years moved along, the United States ended its occupation in August, 1948, and recognized the Republic of Korea below the Thirty-eighth Parallel under President Syngman Rhee, a Princeton-educated Korean. Though MacArthur attended the inauguration of President Rhee, his authority did not extend over this new republic.

While MacArthur was busy with his reforms in Japan, he looked uneasily at Communist gains in the Orient. Besides their activities in North Korea, they had conquered vast China and had chased the Chinese Nationalist government of Chiang Kai-shek to the island of Formosa. Even in Japan, MacArthur was well aware that the Soviet Union was using its well-known tactics to gain control of that country. Had he not made tenant farmers into independent landowners, the rural population would have fallen easy victims of Communist propaganda. The same was true with city workers whom he saved for democracy by permitting them to organize unions.

The Soviet government, which was represented on the Allied Council for Japan, even though it entered the war only a few days before the surrender, nagged constantly for veto power over MacArthur. But he had let them know at the first and only Council meeting he attended that he was boss of the Occupation. When they sought to treat the Emperor as a war criminal, he ignored them. It was his conclusion that the Communists respected strength and firmness and took friendliness as a sign of weakness.

This became clear to his aides when a Soviet official was arrested for leaving Tokyo without a permit. When this man demanded a written apology from MacArthur, the General said sternly, "Tell him there will be no apology, oral or written." On being informed of MacArthur's words, the Russian said in awe, "What a man! He surely is a real leader!"

The Soviet government had 450 Russians in their Tokyo embassy. A majority of them were spies and agitators, and MacArthur kept close watch over them. In addition, the Russians had taken 400,000 Japanese troops in Manchuria and Korea after the surrender. Though MacArthur insisted upon their return to Japan, the Communists had allowed them to dribble back only after a thorough brainwashing. The result was that the Communists could count on a hundred thousand of them to "demonstrate" in Tokyo any time they were ordered.

So far as MacArthur was concerned, the Communists were engaged in "international banditry in Asia." The question was where would they strike next. The answer came on June 25, 1950.

At four A.M. that Sunday, an aide telephoned MacArthur with the news that Communist North Korean armored divisions had rumbled across the Thirty-eighth Parallel. With the invasion of South Korea, MacArthur's first thought was for the safety of 2,000 Americans in Seoul, the capital. Quickly he ordered their immediate evacuation by air.

Although Korea was not under his jurisdiction, MacArthur fully realized that if the United States made no effort to halt the aggressors, her reputation as leader of the free world would be damaged. Even worse, the Reds would interpret this as a sign of weakness. They would later use these same tactics to take over other small countries one by one. He was also sure that if nothing were done, the five-year-old United Nations would reveal itself as a weak organization incapable of protecting its members from aggressors.

From Washington came President Truman's answer: "In these circumstances, I have ordered the United States air and sea forces to give the Korean government troops cover and support." The following day the UN Security Council, with the Soviet Union absent and unable to cast a veto, also took action. It called on member nations to "furnish such assistance to the Republic of Korea as may be necessary to repel the armed attack and restore international peace and security."

When the UN directed the United States to be its agent in Korea, President Truman lost little time asking MacArthur to keep close watch on the situation there. MacArthur had not counted on any further military duty in the field. But, said an aide, "He seemed to have peeled ten years from his shoulders." He walked and talked more quickly and his eyes took on renewed fire.

The news from Korea was immediately bad. The capital city of Seoul had already fallen and President Rhee had moved his government to Taejon, about halfway down to Pusan at the southern tip of his country. From the thrust and speed of the North Korean Communists, MacArthur was concerned that they would soon overrun the entire area below the Thirty-eighth Parallel.

There was only one way to judge the fighting between the North Koreans and the Republic of Korea's (ROK) forces. MacArthur would go to the front and find out for himself. As he said, "You can only tell how an army is fighting by being up with the men at the front."

In a rainstorm MacArthur took off in his unarmed *Bataan* on June 28 from Tokyo's airport for Korea. "He walked halfway to Korea with his continual pacing of the aisle," said his pilot. In his mouth was the stem of his corncob pipe as he puffed small clouds of smoke. "I don't dare smoke this back in Tokyo," he said to a reporter who had come with him. "If I did the people would think I was a farmer." Over Korea, a Russian Yak fighter came at his plane. But four American Mustangs had risen to escort the *Bataan,* and the Yak finally zoomed away.

On landing at Suwon, twenty miles south of Seoul, Mac-Arthur was given a military briefing. Dissatisfied, he said, "Let's go see the troops in action."

In jeeps he and several aides drove to the south bank of the Han River, only a mile below Seoul. The city ahead lay burning. Red airplanes were strafing the area. All the roads leading south from Seoul were crowded with fleeing women and children. Of the ROK Army of 96,000 men, more than half were already killed, wounded or taken prisoner. The ROK forces had been trained more for police duty than for warfare. In their haste to get across the Han, they had blown up several bridges and trapped their own men on the wrong side of the river. Through his field glasses, MacArthur watched the six North Korean divisions and their hundred Russian tanks and heavy artillery move about wherever they wished.

"It is as efficient and as able a force as I've ever seen in the field," he concluded.

On the way back to Suwon, the jeeps were attacked from the air. While everyone headed for ditches, MacArthur stood alongside the road and stared angrily at the strafing planes. One of the jeeps was badly hit by enemy fire, but no one in MacArthur's group was injured.

His mind was made up by the time the *Bataan* returned to Tokyo. The Republic of Korea could not be saved by the United States or the UN if aid were restricted to air and sea support, as President Truman had ordered. For the ROK Army had almost vanished and what remained was in full retreat. The decision on what to do now would be up to President Truman.

During the evening of June 30th, MacArthur held a telecon (teletype radio conference) with the Joint Chiefs of Staff at the Pentagon. "The South Korean forces are in confusion, have not seriously fought and lack leadership," he said. "If the enemy advances continue much further, it will threaten the Republic." Now he made his important recommendation. The only way to prevent the complete defeat of the South Koreans would be to send "United States ground combat forces into the Korean battle area."

Within hours President Truman accepted his recommendation. MacArthur was to send in ground troops from his occupation force in Japan to stem the Communist tide. A few days later he was notified that he had been appointed Commander in Chief of the United Nations Forces in Korea. "I hope I will not fail you," was his reply to President Truman. Yet he knew how desperate the situation had become.

In Japan, MacArthur had only four infantry divisions,

and these were at far from full strength. They were occupation troops and untrained for combat. Moreover, the question arose whether he could safely remove his occupation troops from Japan and still retain his authority as Supreme Commander. In time three of the divisions went to Korea. Said MacArthur: "The reaction of the Japanese was magnificent. They not only morally and spiritually supported everything we did, but all of the incidental friction of democracy, such as labor struggles, ceased at once without any word from me."

A basic principle of warfare is never to send troops into a fight in small groups. Military academies throughout the world teach that piecemeal use of troops is fatal, for a large enemy army can surround, cut up and destroy without trace weak, isolated troops. MacArthur knew this well, but he also believed he had no alternative. "We must trade lives for time," he said grimly. However, deep within him, he hoped that his understanding of the Oriental mind would lead the North Koreans to misinterpret what he was doing.

This one chance in a million succeeded. MacArthur described what happened when he sent isolated small groups of American soldiers to withstand enemy tank divisions: "I threw in troops by air in the hope of establishing a locus of resistance around which I could rally the fast retreating South Korean forces. I also hoped by that arrogant display to fool the enemy into a belief that I had greater resources at my disposal than I did.

"I managed to throw in a part of two battalions of infantry who put up a magnificent resistance before they were destroyed, a resistance which resulted, perhaps, in one of the most vital successes that we had. The enemy undoubtedly could not understand that we could make such an effort with such a small force. Instead of rushing rapidly forward to Pusan, which he could have reached within a week, without the slightest difficulty, he stopped to deploy his artillery across the Han. We gained ten days by that process."

This piecemeal commitment gave MacArthur the time he needed to bring in two divisions from Japan. During those precious days when the North Koreans, who outnumbered the Americans a hundred to one, spread their troops at the Han for an expected large battle, MacArthur's staff in Tokyo went on twenty-four-hours-a-day duty. With lightning speed, men and equipment were poured into ships and planes. By the time the Communists realized what had happened, MacArthur's forces had grouped themselves at the southern tip of Korea around the port of Pusan.

Nevertheless, when the North Koreans again began moving toward Pusan, they vastly outnumbered the American-Korean forces. There was still a good chance that they eventually would take Pusan and push the Americans into the sea. By mid-July they were fast on the move. Lieutenant General Walton Walker's Eighth Army stood before them not far above Pusan at Taegu. "Stand or die!" he ordered his troops. "There will be no more retreating." By the nineteenth, MacArthur was able to inform President Truman, "We have bought the precious time necessary to build a secure base."

Throughout August, the North Koreans continued their strong pressure against the Pusan beachhead. It became obvious to MacArthur that Walker's army was grimly holding on, but no more. Something spectacular was needed to save the situation.

On a flight over enemy-held territory in South Korea, MacArthur had looked down toward the ground and seen that the rice crop was about ready for harvesting. "We must get that crop and not let the North Koreans have it," he said determinedly.

Then one night not long afterward he read an account of the campaign made by British General James Wolfe in 1759 to take the French walled city of Quebec. Wolfe's entire staff argued that an attack up the steep riverbanks to the south of Quebec could not succeed. It would not be possible to scale those heights. But, said Wolfe, if his staff thought that such an attack was impossible, so would the French. By doing just this, Wolfe took French General Montcalm by surprise and captured Quebec.

What Wolfe did in the French and Indian War, MacArthur would do in Korea. He would find the one place where his staff believed successful action was impossible. If his own aides believed this, so would the enemy. Such an attack would then come as a complete surprise to the Communists.

The place MacArthur selected for an amphibious landing was at Inchon, on the west Korean coast near Seoul and almost back to the Thirty-eighth Parallel. The North Koreans would never expect him to attack so far to their rear. Moreover, Inchon offered the most hazardous spot for an amphibious landing. The tides there were the highest in the Far East. Their average rise and fall was more than twenty feet. Because of their movement, any landing would have to be made at high tide, and even then there would be only a few hours to complete the task.

When MacArthur informed the Pentagon that he planned an amphibious landing at Inchon, the Joint Chiefs of Staff frowned upon his proposal. "The alternative is a frontal attack," he replied. When he persisted with a further request for Inchon, General J. Lawton Collins, Army Chief óf Staff, and Admiral Forrest Sherman, Chief of Naval Operations, came to Tokyo to talk him out of it.

The meeting took place at the Dai-Ichi Building on August 23. Staff aides of Admiral Sherman presented the Navy's case against the landing. They pointed to the tides and also to the narrow, winding channel there. If a single ship were sunk, it would block the channel to all other vessels. They also noted that within a few hours after high tide, there would be no water two miles from shore. Ships still there would be caught in mud and would be easy targets for shore batteries.

General Collins argued that Inchon was too far behind the Pusan zone to relieve pressure on that area. In addition, it was believed that the Communists had large forces in Seoul close by. What Collins proposed was that MacArthur give up his notion of Inchon and land at a safer place farther south, such as Kunsan.

MacArthur was quiet for a long while after the arguments ended. Finally he said, "The very arguments you make as to the impracticabilities involved will tend to insure for me the element of surprise. For the enemy commander will reason that no one would be so brash as to make such an attempt." As for a landing at Kunsan, he went on, it would be safer but "it would not sever the enemy's supply lines or distribution center and would therefore serve little purpose."

He turned to the gathering. "The only alternative to a stroke such as I propose would be a continuation of the savage sacrifice we are making at Pusan, with no hope of relief in sight. Are you content to let our troops stay in that bloody perimeter like beef cattle in the slaughterhouse?

Who would take the responsibility for such a tragedy? Certainly I will not.

"The prestige of the Western World hangs in the balance," he went on. "Oriental millions are watching the outcome. It is apparent that here in Asia the Communist conspirators have elected to make their play for global conquest. . . . Make the wrong decision here and we will be done." As for Inchon, he said finally, "It will save a hundred thousand lives."

Neither the admiral nor the general told him they favored Inchon when the meeting ended. However, six days later MacArthur got a telegram from the Pentagon. "We concur," it read.

The Inchon landing came on September 15. After a softening by naval guns, Inchon saw the success of the Marine assault waves. MacArthur strode on shore and noted with satisfaction how the enemy had been taken by complete surprise.

By September 28, Seoul fell to MacArthur's forces. Quickly he restored the government of President Rhee. Hard pressed within the Pusan beachhead, General Walker noticed that the enemy's strength had suddenly weakened. When the North Koreans tried to turn north, MacArthur ordered their supply lines cut. Pressed now from the north and from the south, the Communist forces rapidly disintegrated. About 130,000 North Koreans were taken prisoner as MacArthur's men retook the entire area below the Thirty-eighth Parallel. From Washington came President Truman's message: "I speak for the entire American people when I send you my warmest congratulations on the victory achieved under your leadership. Few operations in military history can match either the delaying actions where you traded space for time, or the brilliant maneuver which has resulted in the liberation of Seoul."

With the clearing of the North Korean Communists from the area below the Thirty-eighth Parallel, the situation had returned to what it had been before June 25. Would this now be the end of the fighting?

Late that September, General Chung Il Kwon, the Korean Army Chief of Staff, got a call from MacArthur saying he was not to cross above the Thirty-eighth Parallel until there had been a UN decision. The following day President Rhee ordered Chung to cross the Parallel. It was on October 2nd when MacArthur was notified by the Joint Chiefs of Staff to proceed across the Thirty-eighth Parallel and liberate all of Korea to its northern boundary at the Yalu River.

On October 7 approval came from the UN and Mac-Arthur sent his forces northward. However, before he did so, he issued two cease-fire appeals to Communist leaders of North Korea. The second appeal contained the following ultimatum: "I, as the United Nations Commander in Chief, for the last time call upon you to lay down your arms and cease hostilities . . . and cooperate in establishing a unified, independent and democratic government." When no reply came, he sent his forces across the Parallel "to destroy the North Korean army and unify the entire nation."

MacArthur had won the first war in Korea by regaining control up to the Thirty-eighth Parallel. He was now to become involved in a stalemate in the second war in Korea through the intervention of Chinese Communists.

With typical brilliance, MacArthur's military program in North Korea operated with clockwork precision. The Eighth Army under General Walker began a drive up the center of North Korea to Pyongyang, the Communist capital. In the meantime, the X Corps under Lieutenant General Edward N. (Ned) Almond moved up the east coast. Token troop units of sixteen member nations of the UN were also included in the forces driving north, as were strong ROK troop forces from South Korea.

President Truman had never met General MacArthur, and now as the drive to the Yalu River frontier with Manchuria got underway, he requested MacArthur to meet with him.

They met at Wake Island at six o'clock in the morning on October 15. MacArthur had walked his plane's aisle all eight hours of his flight from Tokyo and he had slept only an hour and a half, after landing. "I've been a long time meeting you," said President Truman upon shaking hands. In a banged-up old car, the best on the island, they drove to a Quonset hut in the burning heat.

Their first talk, which lasted an hour, took place between the President and General alone. A second meeting shortly afterward included advisers of both men. MacArthur had paid a call on Chiang Kai-shek at Formosa some time earlier and had issued a strong statement about defending Formosa. At his private meeting with President Truman, MacArthur apologized for his Formosa statement if he had in any way appeared to overstep his military authority. Truman accepted his comment good-naturedly.

At the second meeting, the two went into several questions. Both considered it time to draw up a Japanese peace treaty. They also discussed postwar rebuilding of Korea. Toward the end of this meeting, the President asked MacArthur, "What are the chances for Chinese or Soviet interference in the Korean fighting?"

MacArthur's reply was that he could only guess, but that

he thought there was small chance of Chinese Communist troop aid to the North Koreans against him. He pointed out that this was the information supplied him by the State Department, Defense Department, and the Central Intelligence Agency. No one present from those agencies argued with his reply, and the meeting broke up on cordial terms.

Once again MacArthur returned to the Korean War. The vital North Korean port city of Wonsan fell after an amphibious action of General Almond's X Corps. However, almost two weeks were wasted here clearing the harbor of floating mines.

On October 20, the North Korean capital of Pyongyang fell to General Walker. As in New Guinea, MacArthur used paratroopers to surprise the enemy. The drop was made twenty-five miles north of the capital. At the same time, ground troops moved on the city from the other side. MacArthur had gone along by plane to witness the paratroop drop. Shortly afterward when he entered Pyongyang, almost the entire population turned out to greet his army with wild enthusiasm.

So far as MacArthur's trained military mind could see, the war was over except for a minor mopping-up job. Without any loss of time, he ordered the North Korean commander to surrender and to "liberate all UN prisoners of war and civilian internees and to make adequate provision for their protection, care and maintenance." Throughout the fighting he had seen evidence of the brutal murder of young American prisoners of war by the North Koreans.

When no reply came to his order, MacArthur wondered why. He had told President Truman that intelligence reports had stated the presence of more than 300,000 Chinese Red troops in Manchuria across the Yalu. Could the fact that the Chinese Reds were now planning to enter the war have brought about the refusal of the North Korean commander to surrender?

With some concern about this possibility, he decided to see for himself. In an unarmed plane, he flew the entire length of the Yalu. Down below, he saw no troop concentrations. There was only ice and snow over the barren landscape.

The blow soon fell. A single Chinese prisoner was captured on October 26. A few days later sixteen Chinese prisoners were taken. Other Chinese soldiers were taken by the various armies under MacArthur, but all claimed to be "volunteers" and not part of a regular Chinese invasion force. Communist ground resistance stiffened while Russian-built planes flew across to Korea from Manchuria and bombed UN troops. MacArthur requested the right of "hot pursuit," or the right of his planes to chase invading planes over the air of Manchuria. Although the American government approved, UN Allies did not on the ground that this would spread the war. Accordingly, MacArthur was forbidden to make any "hot pursuit."

Suddenly most of the Chinese "volunteers" mysteriously disappeared from the fighting forces in North Korea. Slowly, in the face of winter, MacArthur's men began a renewed drive toward the Yalu. On November 21, they reached the border. MacArthur flew in for a personal inspection. He looked with concern at the bridges over the Yalu leading from Manchuria to Korea. He had requested permission to destroy these bridges, but he had been denied. However, the fighting would soon be over if the Chinese Communists did not join the war in strength. On November 24, he called for a final offensive and said: "If successful this should for all practical purposes end the war, restore peace and unity to Korea . . . [and] enable the prompt withdrawal of United Nations military forces."

Only two days later, on November 26, MacArthur's dream of victory disappeared. Across the planks of the Yalu River bridges, more than 200,000 well-trained and armed Chinese Communist soldiers had marched under cover of darkness. With a rush, they overwhelmed ROK forces near the border as they came down the central sector. Soon they were thirty miles behind the UN front lines and cut supply lines and blocked roads.

Though he had not expected a Chinese invasion, MacArthur had made plans for it nevertheless. What was not anticipated was that the Chinese Reds would make frontal attacks in human waves, without regard to casualties until by sheer numbers they would overwhelm his men.

Pyongyang fell. By January 4, 1951, Seoul also fell and MacArthur regrouped his forces to new positions running east and west seventy miles below the Thirty-eighth Parallel. For a while it had looked as if his troops would be driven once more back to Pusan at the southern tip and then perhaps forced to evacuate. But his men held at their new positions, and by the end of the month they slowly started northward again. Much of the credit for this forward movement was due to General Matthew B. Ridgway, who had taken command of the Eighth Army when General Walker was killed in a jeep accident.

In March, MacArthur's forces were back again at the Thirty-eighth Parallel. The fighting had become what he called "the accordion war." First one side advanced a little and then the other side began an offensive. The Chinese

Reds still attacked in waves and threw away tens of thousands of lives without concern.

MacArthur viewed this bloody stalemate with horror. Such fighting could produce no victory and yet it went on at "tremendous expense of American blood." He saw no excuse for the government's new policy of a war of attrition, one intended to wear out the enemy with long-drawn-out and little-by-little actions.

A half century before, MacArthur's father, General Arthur MacArthur, had taken a stand in opposition to civilian policy in the Philippines. For this he had been relieved of duty and recalled home. His son was to repeat his experience now.

Publicly, General Douglas MacArthur began to write and speak out against his government's policy of a war of attrition. He complained of the enemy's "privileged sanctuary" behind the Yalu which he was not permitted to bomb. He called for a blockade of the coast of China, air bombardment of her industrial centers and the use of Chiang Kai-shek's military forces on Formosa. Such action, he insisted, would end Chinese pressure on his forces inside Korea and would "severely cripple and largely neutralize China's capability to wage aggressive warfare."

President Truman believed that these proposals would only lead the United States into a mammoth war with China. "What would suit the ambitions of the Kremlin better," Truman said, "than for our military forces to be committed to a full-scale war with Red China?" Such a conflict, he maintained, would involve his country "in the wrong war, at the wrong place, at the wrong time and with the wrong enemy."

It was not long before President Truman concluded that General MacArthur was appealing to the American people over the head of the President of the United States. He insisted that such public appeals only served to weaken the President's constitutional authority over the military branch of government.

On April 11, 1951, General and Mrs. MacArthur were eating lunch with two guests in the American Embassy in Tokyo. Mrs. MacArthur glanced toward the doorway and spied the tearful face of one of her husband's aides. Quickly she begged to be excused and hurried to see what was wrong with the man.

He told her that news had just come over the radio that President Truman had removed MacArthur from his command. The President had said: "With deep regret I have concluded that General of the Army Douglas MacArthur is unable to give his wholehearted support to the policies of the United States Government and of the United Nations. . . . The nation owes him a debt of gratitude for the distinguished and exceptional service which he has rendered his country in posts of great responsibility. For that reason I repeat my regret at the necessity for the action."

When Mrs. MacArthur walked back into the dining room, her husband was laughing at a humorous remark made by one of the guests. She bent over him and whispered the news in his ear. His face grew stiff and he was silent for a long moment. Then he glanced up at his wife and in a soft voice he said, "Jeannie, we are going home at last."